OPPOSING
VIEWPOINTS®
SERIES

# Teen Drug Abuse

JUN '07

MAY '07

JUN 10

'07

# Other Books of Related Interest:

## Opposing Viewpoints Series

Addiction

Advertising

America's Youth

Chemical Dependency

Drug Abuse

Marijuana

Tobacco and Smoking

Teens at Risk

## Current Controversies Series

Alcoholism

Drug Abuse

Drug Legalization

Illegal Drugs

Smoking

Teen Addiction

Teens and Alcohol

## At Issue Series

Alcohol Abuse

Are Americans Overmedicated?

Attention Deficit Hyperactivity Disorder

Does Advertising Promote Substance Abuse?

Drug Testing

Drunk Driving

Heroin

Legalizing Drugs

Smoking

Teen Smoking

"Congress shall make no law . . . abridging the freedom of speech, or of the press."

*First Amendment to the U.S. Constitution*

The basic foundation of our democracy is the First Amendment guarantee of freedom of expression. The Opposing Viewpoints Series is dedicated to the concept of this basic freedom and the idea that it is more important to practice it than to enshrine it.

OPPOSING
VIEWPOINTS®
SERIES

# Teen Drug Abuse

*Pamela Willwerth Aue, Book Editor*

**GREENHAVEN PRESS**
*An imprint of Thomson Gale, a part of The Thomson Corporation*

THOMSON

GALE

Detroit • New York • San Francisco • New Haven, Conn. • Waterville, Maine • London • Munich

Bonnie Szumski, *Publisher*
Helen Cothran, *Managing Editor*

*For more information, contact:* Greenhaven Press
27500 Drake Rd.
Farmington Hills, MI 48331-3535
Or you can visit our Internet site at http://www.gale.com

**LIBRARY OF CONGRESS CATALOGING-IN-PUBLICATION DATA**

Library of Congress Control Number: 2006904381

Printed in the United States of America
10 9 8 7 6 5 4 3 2 1

# Contents

## Chapter 3: Do the Media Promote Teen Drug Abuse?

# Why Consider Opposing Viewpoints?

> *"The only way in which a human being can make some approach to knowing the whole of a subject is by hearing what can be said about it by persons of every variety of opinion and studying all modes in which it can be looked at by every character of mind. No wise man ever acquired his wisdom in any mode but this."*
>
> *John Stuart Mill*

In our media-intensive culture it is not difficult to find differing opinions. Thousands of newspapers and magazines and dozens of radio and television talk shows resound with differing points of view. The difficulty lies in deciding which opinion to agree with and which "experts" seem the most credible. The more inundated we become with differing opinions and claims, the more essential it is to hone critical reading and thinking skills to evaluate these ideas. Opposing Viewpoints books address this problem directly by presenting stimulating debates that can be used to enhance and teach these skills. The varied opinions contained in each book examine many different aspects of a single issue. While examining these conveniently edited opposing views, readers can develop critical thinking skills such as the ability to compare and contrast authors' credibility, facts, argumentation styles, use of persuasive techniques, and other stylistic tools. In short, the Opposing Viewpoints Series is an ideal way to attain the higher-level thinking and reading skills so essential in a culture of diverse and contradictory opinions.

In addition to providing a tool for critical thinking, Opposing Viewpoints books challenge readers to question their own strongly held opinions and assumptions. Most people form their opinions on the basis of upbringing, peer pressure, and personal, cultural, or professional bias. By reading carefully balanced opposing views, readers must directly confront new ideas as well as the opinions of those with whom they disagree. This is not to simplistically argue that everyone who reads opposing views will—or should—change his or her opinion. Instead, the series enhances readers' understanding of their own views by encouraging confrontation with opposing ideas. Careful examination of others' views can lead to the readers' understanding of the logical inconsistencies in their own opinions, perspective on why they hold an opinion, and the consideration of the possibility that their opinion requires further evaluation.

## Evaluating Other Opinions

To ensure that this type of examination occurs, Opposing Viewpoints books present all types of opinions. Prominent spokespeople on different sides of each issue as well as well-known professionals from many disciplines challenge the reader. An additional goal of the series is to provide a forum for other, less known, or even unpopular viewpoints. The opinion of an ordinary person who has had to make the decision to cut off life support from a terminally ill relative, for example, may be just as valuable and provide just as much insight as a medical ethicist's professional opinion. The editors have two additional purposes in including these less known views. One, the editors encourage readers to respect others' opinions—even when not enhanced by professional credibility. It is only by reading or listening to and objectively evaluating others' ideas that one can determine whether they are worthy of consideration. Two, the inclusion of such viewpoints encourages the important critical thinking skill of objectively evaluating an author's credentials and bias. This evaluation will illuminate an author's reasons for taking a particular stance on an issue and will aid in readers' evaluation of the author's ideas.

It is our hope that these books will give readers a deeper understanding of the issues debated and an appreciation of the complexity of even seemingly simple issues when good and honest people disagree. This awareness is particularly important in a democratic society such as ours in which people enter into public debate to determine the common good. Those with whom one disagrees should not be regarded as enemies but rather as people whose views deserve careful examination and may shed light on one's own.

Thomas Jefferson once said that "difference of opinion leads to inquiry, and inquiry to truth." Jefferson, a broadly educated man, argued that "if a nation expects to be ignorant and free. . .it expects what never was and never will be." As individuals and as a nation, it is imperative that we consider the opinions of others and examine them with skill and discernment. The Opposing Viewpoints Series is intended to help readers achieve this goal.

*David L. Bender and Bruno Leone,*
*Founders*

# Introduction

*"If aliens landed on Earth and watched TV for an hour, they'd no doubt conclude that Americans are the most drug-dependent creatures in the universe. Advertisements for prescription drugs are fired out like baseballs in a batting cage. Trouble sleeping? Take Ambien! High cholesterol? Try Zocor! Heartburn? Ask about Nexium!"*

—Anita Manning, USA Today, February 14, 2005

In both 2004 and 2005, the results of Monitoring the Future, an annual survey of youth behavior, showed continuing declines in the use of street drugs, including marijuana. This was touted as proof that the nation's costly drug abuse prevention efforts are achieving success. However, the surveys also revealed that the recreational use of prescription pharmaceuticals and over-the-counter (OTC) drugs by teens is rising. Observers say that one reason for this is that drugs purchased from a pharmacy are believed to be less dangerous than traditional street drugs. Nora Volkow, director of the National Institute on Drug Abuse (NIDA), also notes that these drugs are easily available and socially acceptable. "They become part of our everyday lives," says Volkow. "You see an ad for medication the way you see an ad for shampoo, and the message is that it's just like an everyday thing."

The U.S. Food and Drug Administration loosened restrictions on direct-to-consumer advertising of prescription drugs in 1997. Since then, American consumers have been deluged by television, radio, Internet, and print ads for products they can purchase via a prescription from a doctor. Treatments for allergies, anxiety, arthritis, asthma, and attention deficit disorder are advertised alongside pills to reduce cholesterol, depression, heart disease, insomnia, and sexual dysfunction. Widely advertised drugs also include nonprescription OTC cures for headaches, fevers, muscle strain, cold symptoms, constipation (and its distant cousin, diarrhea), indigestion, and athlete's foot. The message is, "There's a safe and effective pill for every ill; see your doctor or pharmacist and feel better now!"

Advertisers evidently believe that consumers want to hear this message, and drug companies are willing to pay plenty to get the word out. In 2001 major pharmaceutical companies spent more than $19 billion promoting their products, of which nearly $3 billion was spent on direct-to-consumer advertising. This was a dramatic increase from 1996's consumer promotion spending of $800 million. Apparently, spending on such advertising is working. In 2004 consumers and their insurance companies spent $180 billion on prescription medications. In December 2004 the Centers for Disease Control and Prevention (CDC) reported that consumer spending on drugs has risen 15 percent or more every year since 1998.

The legitimate use of prescription drugs has increased dramatically since the early 1990s for Americans of all ages. According to Greg Critser, author of *Generation Rx: How Prescription Drugs Are Altering American Lives, Minds, and Bodies*, the average number of drugs prescribed per person in 1993 was seven. By 2004 the average had risen to twelve per person per year. The CDC reports that in 2000, 44 percent of Americans used at least one prescription drug on a regular basis and 17 percent used three or more. Among children and adolescents the use of prescription drugs has become quite commonplace as well. Between 1994 and 2001 the childhood use of antibiotics rose 4.3 percent, while the use of asthma treatment drugs went up 15 percent, antidepressants up 21 percent, and gastrointestinal distress drugs up 28 percent. Teens' use of psychotropic prescription drugs—those prescribed for attention deficit/hyperactivity disorder (ADHD), depression, and anxiety disorders—increased 250 percent.

The use of carefully administered prescription drugs and inexpensive OTC remedies improves both the quality and longevity of life for millions of Americans. However, an unintended consequence of the proliferation of ever more powerful pharmaceuticals is the use of otherwise legal drugs for illegal purposes. According to NIDA, prescription drugs are intentionally misused by approximately 6 million adults in the United States. In some cases dependency and addiction follow the legitimate use of a drug. A different type of abuse occurs when users discover what is known in the drug industry as an "off-label" use of a prescription drug, as in the case of college students without ADHD who buy Ritalin from friends with legitimate prescriptions because the pills help them stay awake to cram for exams.

Today's teens and young adults may be less willing to experiment with traditional street drugs than were previous generations, but they are just as inclined to turn to pills and potions in the hope of finding happiness, peer acceptance, stress relief, or an escape from reality. Says NIDA director Volkow, "When it comes to adolescents, we're used to worrying about illegal drugs, but we have to also be worried about the legal ones." The proliferation of prescription and OTC drugs, and the direct-to-consumer ads promoting them, have encouraged many teens to shift from using illegal substances to legal ones. Not only are the legal drugs more accessible, but because they are advertised on TV and used openly by family members and friends, these substances appear harmless.

Counselors and other experts involved in drug treatment and prevention are scrambling to catch up with the trend.

Strategies that worked when teens were using illicit drugs do not necessarily work to address abuse of prescription and OTC drugs. In *Opposing Viewpoints: Teen Drug Abuse*, authors debate current teen substance abuse trends in the following chapters: Is Teen Drug Abuse a Serious Problem? What Causes Teen Drug Abuse? Do the Media Promote Teen Drug Abuse? How Can Teen Drug Abuse Be Prevented? The many viewpoints included in this volume demonstrate that teen drug abuse is a complex personal, social, and political issue that will continue to offer much opportunity for debate.

# CHAPTER 1

# Is Teen Drug Abuse a Serious Problem?

# Chapter Preface

Results from the 2005 Monitoring the Future Survey, which were released in December 2005, suggest that alcohol use among high school seniors has decreased significantly during the past thirty years. In 1975 nearly 85 percent of seniors reported having used alcohol during the previous year; in 2005, 68.6 percent reported drinking in the last year. This is good news, of course, but statistics still indicate that more than two-thirds of high school seniors, who are usually three years away from the age of legal consumption, engage in some level of alcohol use. Researchers investigating substance use often ask, "How many of these underage drinkers will develop alcohol dependency?" And, "Are the occasional drinkers *using* alcohol or are they *abusing* it?"

At a time when abstinence-only, "zero tolerance" policies dominate the drug education landscape, it may seem inappropriate to draw a distinction between teen drug use and teen drug abuse. Many people feel strongly that any kind of drug use among teens constitutes abuse. When it comes to illicit drugs or underage smoking and drinking, of course, there is no such thing as a legally acceptable level of use: All such use is illegal. Treatment professionals note, however, that in order to understand the scope and nature of teen substance abuse, and to create effective preventive or treatment measures, it is important to recognize that there are differences between experimental users and those who develop addictions. In other words, many experts contend that teen drug use does not automatically equate with drug abuse.

Susan M. Gordon, director of research and professional training at the Caron Foundation, which offers addiction treatment to teens and adults, notes that most adolescents who try drugs or alcohol do not become addicted to any substance. In light of that fact, she writes, "to develop successful prevention programs it is necessary to understand why some teens never experiment and others stop experimenting with drugs before their use becomes abuse, and why some teens continue experimentation and drug abuse despite negative consequences."

The Caron Foundation has found that addicted teens are more likely than nonaddicted teens to suffer from attention deficit/hyperactivity disorder (ADHD) as well as severe anxiety, depression, and eating disorders. Caron professionals also have found that teens with addictions frequently come from homes where parents—whether intentionally or not—encourage teen substance abuse. In many cases, alcohol and tobacco are easily accessible to teens, and parents may consider underage use acceptable. Easy access to painkillers or other prescription drugs can also lead to addiction, Caron experts found. Many parents simply do not realize the addictive potential of these drugs and do not take steps to secure them. Finally, a lack of strong parental connection and presence in the lives of adolescents is a common factor among teens who move from experimentation to addiction.

These findings do not mean that kids who live in tightly supervised homes, in which alcohol and prescription drugs are locked up, are immune to psychological problems and drug dependency. However, it does suggest that not all teens are equally susceptible to addiction. Many researchers contend that it is important to acknowledge that there may be underlying differences in the personal lives of occasional users compared with the lives of those developing addictions to drugs. By acknowledging these differences these experts are not implying that there is an acceptable level of use. Rather, they claim it is an important step toward creating effective prevention and treatment programs. They point out that viewing all teen drug users as exactly alike runs the risk of neglecting the critical factors that can transform a teen from a user to an abuser.

Authors examine this issue further in the following chapter. Deciding whether or not teen drug abuse is a serious problem is not, as the Caron Foundation discovered, simply a matter of gathering statistics. Equally important, the researchers note, is distinguishing between use and abuse, and identifying the factors that lead to addiction.

| "*[The government] announced a 9 percent decline in illicit drug use among American youth . . . from 2002 to 2004.*"

# Teen Drug Abuse Is Decreasing

## *Office of National Drug Control Policy*

*The following viewpoint presents the results of the 2004 National Survey on Drug Use and Health (NSDUH), conducted by the Substance Abuse and Mental Health Services Administration, a federal agency. A key finding of the report is that teen use of illicit drugs such as marijuana, methamphetamines, and cocaine has decreased. Teen use of alcohol and tobacco also declined, according to the report. The findings of the report are summarized by the Office of National Drug Control Policy, a White House agency established by the Anti-Drug Abuse Act of 1988 to establish policies and strategies for reducing the use, manufacturing, and trafficking of illicit drugs.*

As you read, consider the following questions:

    1. According to the NSDUH report, what are the differ-

Office of National Drug Control Policy, "Youth Drug Use Continues to Decline," 2005.

ences in the rate of marijuana use among boys between 12 and 17 and among girls in the same age range?

2. To what factors does Charles Curie attribute the statistical drop in illicit drug use among American teens, as cited by the author?

3. According to the NSDUH report, which family life behaviors are linked to the rate of teen use of illicit drugs, alcohol, and tobacco?

Health and Human Services [HHS] Secretary Mike Leavitt announced a 9 percent decline in illicit drug use among American youth between the ages of 12 and 17 from 2002 to 2004. Marijuana use also declined by 7 percent among young adults between the ages of 18 and 25 during this same period. Marijuana continues to be the most commonly used illicit drug, with a rate of 6.1 percent (14.6 million current users) for the U.S. population 12 and older. The findings are from the 2004 National Survey on Drug Use and Health (NSDUH) released today [September 8, 2005] at the annual National Alcohol and Drug Addiction Recovery Month press conference.

## Survey Findings

The survey findings, released by HHS' Substance Abuse and Mental Health Services Administration (SAMHSA), show that overall 19.1 million Americans, or 7.9 percent of the population ages 12 and older were current illicit drug users, meaning they used an illicit drug in the past month. This rate was similar to the rates seen in 2002 and 2003, around 8 percent of the population ages 12 and older.

Particularly striking was a decline in current use, defined as used in the past month, of marijuana among boys ages 12–17, from 9.1 percent in 2002 down to 8.1 percent in 2004. But marijuana use by girls in that age group did not decline and remained at about 7 percent. Similarly, for the 18–25 year old category, the cohort with the highest illicit drug use rates, there were declines in current marijuana use from 17.3 percent in 2002 to 16.1 percent in 2004; and use of hallucinogens from 1.9 percent in 2002 to 1.5 percent in 2004 . . . .

"This is very encouraging news," said John P. Walters, Director of National Drug Control Policy. "Our balanced drug control strategy is paying off—especially in the most important category: young people. We need to follow through in certain areas: rising prescription drug abuse and continued flat rates of adult methamphetamine use that we need to push down. But, today's survey confirms the welcome trend on teen drug use. We know that reductions in youth drug use now pay large dividends in reducing the future human and economic costs of drug use to our nation."

An area of concern is the increasing non-medical use of prescription medications among young adults. The 2004 survey shows about 6 percent of young adults used medications non-medically in the past month, and 29 percent had used [them] in their lifetime. From 2002 to 2004 there was an increase in lifetime prevalence of non-medical use of narcotic pain relievers in the 18–25 age group, from 22 percent to 24 percent. Hydrocodone and oxycodone products showed increases in lifetime use among young adults ages 18 to 25.

"The news today is an indication that our partnerships and the work of prevention professionals, schools, parents, teachers, law enforcement, religious leaders, and local community anti-drug coalitions are paying off," SAMHSA Administrator Charles Curie said. "Yet our work is far from over. We must continue our efforts to support people in their struggle with substance abuse and mental illness to help ensure they have the opportunity for recovery."

## Marijuana and Prescription Drugs

Among persons ages 12 or older who used illicit drugs, 56.8 percent used only marijuana, 19.7 percent used marijuana and

## Changes in Substance Use Among High School Seniors, 1980–2004

| Survey Year | % reporting illegal drug use during previous 30 days | % reporting any marijuana use during past year | % reporting any use of cigarettes during lifetime |
|---|---|---|---|
| 1980 | 37.2 | 48.8 | 71.0 |
| 1983 | 30.5 | 42.3 | 70.6 |
| 1986 | 27.1 | 38.8 | 67.6 |
| 1989 | 19.7 | 29.6 | 65.7 |
| 1992 | 14.4 | 21.9 | 61.8 |
| 1995 | 23.8 | 34.7 | 64.2 |
| 1998 | 25.6 | 37.5 | 65.3 |
| 2001 | 25.7 | 37.0 | 61.0 |
| 2004 | 23.4 | 34.3 | 52.8 |

SOURCE: National Institute on Drug Abuse, "Monitoring the Future: National Survey Results on Drug Use, 1975–2004," 2004.

some other drug and 23.6 percent used only a drug other than marijuana. An estimated 8.2 million persons (3.4 percent of the population ages 12 and older) were current users of illicit drugs other than marijuana in 2004.

In 2004, most of the people using drugs other than marijuana used psychotherapeutic drugs non-medically (6.0 million, 2.5 percent of the population). There were an estimated 4.4 million current users of narcotic pain relievers, 1.6 million users of tranquilizers, 1.2 million used stimulants and 0.3 million used sedatives. These estimates are all similar to the estimates for 2003.

The drug category with the largest number of recent initiates in 2004 was non-medical use of pain relievers (2.4 million new users), followed by marijuana (2.1 million new users), non-medical use of tranquilizers (1.2 million new users) and cocaine (1.0 million new users).

## Methamphetamine, Cocaine, Heroin, and Hallucinogens

Use of methamphetamine remained unchanged from 2002 to 2004 at approximately 5 percent lifetime use and 0.6 percent past-year use, and 0.2 percent for current use. In 2004, 583,000 persons were current users of methamphetamine and 1.4 million persons ages 12 and older used methamphetamine in the past year. The rates of use declined among young people ages 12 to 17.

In 2004 there were an estimated 2.0 million current cocaine users, 0.8 percent of the population ages 12 and older. Of these, 467,000 used crack in the past month (0.2 percent). These estimates are similar to those in 2002 and 2003. Among 12 to 17 year olds, past-year use of cocaine fell 8 percent between 2002 and 2004.

Heroin was used by 0.1 percent of the population ages 12 and older in the past month in 2004. There were 166,000 current heroin users. This is similar to 2002 and 2003. Lifetime heroin use fell 16 percent (from 3.7 million individuals to 3.1 million) between 2003 and 2004.

Hallucinogens were used by 929,000 persons in the past month. The number of current users of Ecstasy ages 12 and older remained the same in 2004 as 2003 after dropping significantly between 2002 and 2003. There were 450,000 current users of Ecstasy in 2004. The rate of current use of other hallucinogens also did not change significantly. The number of past-year users of LSD declined 41 percent between 2002 and 2004, while past-year use of Ecstasy dropped 40 percent over the same time period. Although an estimated 23.4 million persons had tried LSD in their lifetimes, only 141,000 were current users in 2004.

## Alcohol Use

More than one fifth (22.8 percent) of persons ages 12 or older (55 million people) participated in binge drinking at least once in the 30 days prior to being surveyed in 2004. Binge drinking is defined as five or more drinks on the same occasion at least once in the past 30 days. Heavy drinking was reported by 6.9 percent of the population ages 12 and older (16.7 million people). Heavy drinking is defined as five or more drinks on the same occasion on at least five different days in the past 30 days. These figures are similar to estimates in 2002 and 2003.

In 2004, about 10.8 million underage persons ages 12–20 (28.7 percent) reported drinking alcohol in the past month. Nearly 7.4 million were binge drinkers (19.6 percent) and 2.4 million were heavy drinkers (6.3 million). These figures were similar to the 2002 and 2003 estimates.

Among young adults ages 18–25, 41.2 percent engaged in binge drinking and 15.1 percent in heavy alcohol use. The rate of binge and heavy drinking in 2004 peaked at age 21. Among persons ages 65 and older the rates of binge and heavy drinking were lower, 6.9 percent for binge alcohol use and 1.8 percent for heavy drinking.

## Tobacco Use

Rates of current use of a tobacco product declined from 30.4 percent to 29.2 percent between 2002 and 2004. Past-month use of cigarettes decreased from 26.0 to 24.9 percent, while past-month smokeless tobacco use decreased from 3.3 to 3.0 percent between 2002 and 2004. Young adults ages 18–25 had the highest rate of current use of a tobacco product (44.6 percent). Among youth ages 12 to 17, an estimated 3.6 million (14.4 percent) used a tobacco product in the past month in 2004. About three million used cigarettes. The rate of past-month cigarette use in this age group declined from 13.0 percent in 2002 to 11.9 percent in 2004.

## Prevention Measures

In 2004, 60.3 percent of youths aged 12 to 17 reported that they had talked at least once in the past year with at least one of their parents about the dangers of drug, tobacco, or alcohol use. This rate represents an increase from the 2003 rate of 58.9 percent and the 2002 rate of 58.1 percent. Among youths who reported having had such conversations with their parents, rates of current alcohol and cigarette use and past-year and lifetime use of alcohol, cigarettes, and illicit drugs were lower than among youths who did not report such conversations.

In 2004, drug, alcohol, and cigarette use was uniformly lower among youths who reported that their parents always or sometimes engaged in monitoring behaviors such as checking and helping with homework or limiting time spent out on school nights, than among youths whose parents "seldom" or "never" engaged in such behaviors. For instance, for parental assistance with homework, rates of past-month marijuana use were 6.2 percent for youths whose parents always or sometimes helped compared with 14.7 percent among youths indicating their parents seldom or never helped.

*"The number of teenagers who experiment with recreational drugs is nearly the same as it was during its peak years in the early 1970s."*

# The Extent of Teen Drug Abuse Has Not Changed Significantly

*Erik Goldman*

*In the following viewpoint medical journalist Erik Goldman reports on a study conducted by Dr. James Anthony. According to Goldman, recreational drug experimentation among teens has not changed significantly since the early 1970s. Anthony's research suggests that the number of new teen marijuana users, at approximately 2.5 million annually, is nearly identical to the number of new users in the early 1970s. Goldman concludes that the government's anti-drug message, which encourages youths to "just say no," is clearly ineffective.*

As you read, consider the following questions:

1. According to the author, what factors influence the

Erik Goldman, "Teen Drug Use Has Changed Little Since 1970s," in *Family Practice News*, v. 35, no. 6, March 15, 2005, p. 11.

conversion of a recreational drug user to a state of drug dependency?

2. According to Goldman, what does James Anthony say about marijuana as the "gateway" drug?

3. According to Anthony, as cited by Goldman, what are the two major changes in drug use patterns since the 1970s?

The number of teenagers who experiment with recreational drugs is nearly the same as it was during its peak years in the early 1970s, James Anthony, Ph.D., reported at the annual conference of the Association for Research in Nervous and Mental Disease.

Dr. Anthony, who is chairman of the department of epidemiology at Michigan State University, East Lansing, said the trend in the past decade has been approximately 2.5 million new teenage cannabis users each year, an almost identical number as was seen in the early 1970s. The number of people under the age of 18 in the United States is also nearly identical to the figure from the early '70s.

Abuse of prescription drugs such as stimulants, pain relievers, and sedatives appears to be even more common now than it was during the height of the post-1960s "drug culture" era, he noted at the conference, cosponsored by the New York Academy of Medicine.

So much for "Just say no."

## From Experimentation to Addiction

From a public health viewpoint, the important issue is not so much the absolute number of young people who try recreational drugs but the number of new users of those drugs who ultimately become dependent on them. This "conversion" rate from initial use to addiction is influenced by genetics, environmental factors, and most importantly, the nature of the drug itself. The statistics suggest that different substances have very different conversion rates.

According to data from the National Survey on Drug Use and Health (formerly the National Household Survey on Drug Abuse) and the National Comorbidity Survey databases, tobacco is by far the most addictive of the commonly abused substances. One in three individuals who try tobacco will ultimately become dependent on it.

Opiates are a close second, with one in four initial users becoming addicted. Crack and cocaine are next, inducing dependence in one in five and one in six first-time users, respectively. Alcohol causes dependence in one in seven to eight initial users, and stimulants cause dependence in one in nine. For cannabis, the figure is between 1 in 9 and 1 in 11.

Although many drug-avoidance programs aimed at teenagers identify cannabis as the "gateway" drug that leads young people to hard drug use, the statistics suggest that it is tobacco that really should carry that distinction, he said.

Dr. Anthony estimated that there are roughly 4.6 million actively drug-dependent individuals in the United States, and the vast majority go untreated for many years.

Most people who do enter drug treatment programs have been drug dependent for an average of 10 years. In addition to alcohol and tobacco, cocaine is a major contributor to the problem.

"With cocaine, approximately 30% of the general population has the opportunity to try it, but only 50% of those who have the opportunity will try it. For cannabis, 85% of the population has the chance to try it, and 75% end up trying it," he said.

## Drug Use Varies from State to State

Drug use and dependence patterns vary considerably from state to state. For example, estimates of the number of active adult cocaine users vary from 1.8% to 4%, with a U.S. average of 2.5%. The states with the highest prevalence are Nevada, Arizona, Ohio, North Carolina, Massachusetts, and Vermont.

Dr. Anthony said there are roughly 1.1 million new first-time cocaine users in the United States each year.

For cannabis, the number of users varies from 4.3% to 11% of the U.S. population, with an average of 6.2%. The highest-use states include Washington, Oregon, Nevada, Montana, Colorado, Utah, and New Hampshire. He estimated that there are roughly 14.6 million regular users of cannabis across the nation and 2.6 million first-time users each year.

The time frame for development of drug dependence seems to vary considerably for different drugs. With cocaine, between 5% and 6% of first-time users become dependent within the first 2 years of their initial experience. This number rises to more than 16% within 6 years. "The pattern for tobacco looks a lot like cocaine," Dr. Anthony said. With cannabis, between 3% and 4% of those who try the drug become dependent on it within the first 2 years, but the conversion factor drops off markedly after that. In this respect, alcohol is very similar to cannabis.

"If you're not addicted within the first 1 or 2 years, you probably will never be," Dr. Anthony said.

## Biggest Changes in Drug Use Patterns Since the 1970s

Aside from the emergence of ecstasy (3,4-methylenedioxy-methamphetamine) and related substances, the biggest change in patterns of drug abuse since the 1970s has to do with abuse of prescription drugs, particularly stimulants, sedatives, and anti-anxiety drugs. Simply put, there are many more of these kinds of drugs available now, and they are far more widely prescribed than they were. "We're seeing very sharp rises in the numbers [of prescription drug abusers] in all age groups," he said.

Crystal meth (methamphetamine) use has surged, but this trend has very particular regional variances. Often considered the "poor man's cocaine," crystal meth use is quite prevalent in the Southwest, Southern California, and in rural areas of the Midwest.

Although the specific population dynamics surrounding this problem are not entirely understood, Dr. Anthony said he suspects that the economics of drug dealing play a role.

"Wherever you have an entrenched cocaine market, you don't have much of a crystal meth market because of the violence between the cocaine and the meth mobs. Cocaine dealers do not respond very nicely when meth labs start to open up on their turf," he explained.

As in almost all areas of medicine, the genomics revolution has sent many substance abuse researchers deep into the molecular realm in search of specific genes that predispose individuals to drug dependence.

Though he believes this effort is a very important direction for research, Dr. Anthony underscored the need to place equal emphasis on the environmental determinants of addiction.

"The dichotomy between 'enviromics' and genomics is in many ways a false dichotomy. It is not an either/or situation, so we need to take an and/both attitude. Just as we map the genetic material, we ought to be mapping the environmental conditions and processes that shape drug involvement," he said.

*"More American youth drink alcohol
than smoke tobacco or marijuana."*

# Binge Drinking Among Youths Is a Serious Problem

*Jean Weinberg*

*In the following viewpoint Jean Weinberg claims that while the rate of underage drinking has remained steady, episodes of binge drinking increased between 1993 and 2001, particularly among eighteen- to twenty-year-olds. She cites a 2004 study that indicates that slightly more than half of all high school seniors surveyed reported having been drunk during the previous year. She notes that the federal government has renewed its efforts to combat binge drinking. Weinberg is a reporter for CNN.com.*

As you read, consider the following questions:

1. How does the author define binge drinking?

2. What statistical and anecdotal evidence does Weinberg use to support the view that binge drinking is a danger to college students?

3. What solutions does the author present to reduce binge drinking among American youth?

Jean Weinberg, "Under Age, Under the Influence: Efforts Aim to Curb Youth Drinking," in CNN.com, June 6, 2005.

Thirteen years old and in search of a remedy for shyness and a way to bond with friends, Koren Zailckas made alcohol her steady companion.

Drinking heavily on a regular basis, she frequently blacked out. One night, Zailckas had her stomach pumped—waking up in a hospital bed but with no idea how she got there.

"I was drinking and doing stupid things, or drinking and having scary things happen, but then drinking again to . . . mask the memories of it," said Zailckas, now 24, of a cycle that lasted almost a decade.

## Smashed

Statistics suggest Zailckas' story—chronicled in the *New York Times* bestseller "Smashed"—is not uncommon. More American youth drink alcohol than smoke tobacco or marijuana, with drinkers under age 21 accounting for between 12 percent and 20 percent of the U.S. alcohol market (Even the lower estimate, 12 percent, represents 3.6 billion drinkers each year).

The rate of underage drinking has remained fairly constant and, in some cases, dropped: A 2004 Monitoring the Future study indicated that 51.8 percent of 12th graders, 35.1 percent of 10th graders and 14.5 percent of eighth graders reported being drunk in the past year.

## Costs and Consequences of Heavy Drinking

And the costs—financial (between $53 billion and $58 billion annually, according to reports) and healthwise—remain high. This fact makes underage drinking a national problem affecting everyone—not just teens and their parents—advocates of action say.

A late 1990s study from the U.S. Department of Justice linked youth alcohol use to violent crimes that led to damages costing nearly $36 million, vehicle crashes costing more than $18 million, treatment adding up to $2.5 million (including $1.5 million related to suicide attempts) and other expenses.

For all age groups, heavy drinking has been linked to liver damage, memory loss and brain damage, directly contributing to about 6,000 U.S. deaths annually. Other problems include high incidences of crime, traumatic injury (such as car accidents), suicide, fetal alcohol syndrome and alcohol poisoning, according to Mothers Against Drunk Driving [MADD].

Underage drinking has gotten the attention of several members of Congress. Efforts are under way to pass the "The Sober Truth on Preventing Underage Drinking Act" (STOP),[1] which would be the most comprehensive federal legislation on the issue. That bill, which would incur $19 million annually in federal expenditures, has stalled on Capitol Hill, where it faces heated competition for government money.

"We must do all we can to empower parents and communities to protect our youth and to encourage healthy behavior free from binge drinking and other forms of alcohol abuse," said Sen. Jon Corzine, a New Jersey Democrat and bill cosponsor.

## It's Part of the College Experience

Between 1993 and 2001, 18- to 20-year-olds showed the largest increase in binge-drinking episodes (five or more drinks consumed on at least one occasion in the past 30 days) among American adults.

When she went from high school to college, Zailckas said she felt as if it suddenly became all right to consume alcohol.

"If I was in a quiet Friday morning class my teacher would say, 'It all looks like you started your weekend early,'" she said. "It felt like drinking was part of the college experience."

According to the 2000 National Survey on Drug Abuse, the rate of binge drinking was higher among full-time college students (41 percent) than among their peers aged 18 to 22 (38 percent.)

1. The bill, HR 864, was referred to the subcommittee on Health on March 14, 2005, for further study.

## Underage Drinking: Trends and Scope

- Nearly 11 million underage youth, ages 12 to 20, reported drinking in the previous 30 days in 2003.
- More than 7 million underage youth, ages 12 to 20, reported binge drinking in the past 30 days in 2003.
- Underage drinking is estimated to account for between 12% and 20% of the U.S. alcohol market.
- According to calculations using the 2003 National Survey on Drug Use and Health, 13 is the average age at which youth, ages 12 to 17, began drinking.

*Center on Alcohol Marketing and Youth,*
Underage Drinking in the United States, *2004.*

"It is a lot more acceptable in college versus high school," said Jacqueline Hackett, 19, Student of the Year for Students Against Destructive Decisions. "Nobody really has a problem getting drunk on a Wednesday night [in college]. Everyone knows what goes on, and nobody seems to care."

Zailckas said she comprehended the serious dangers of getting severely intoxicated only after leaving the insulated environment of college.

"It was the experience of being around adults instead of students, of being in a strange city instead of a college campus, that really made the dangers of drinking feel real," she said. "That's when I thought there is something really wrong here, there's something wrong with drinking like this, to drinking to just obliteration."

## Legislation to Curb Underage Drinking

The STOP Act, reintroduced February 16 [2005] (having originally been brought up in July 2004), would coordinate government efforts to curb alcohol consumption by minors.

The legislation would mandate cooperation between federal agencies, increase prevention activities in states and municipalities, finance a public service media campaign and support related research.

"The STOP Underage Drinking Act will provide the resources necessary to educate young people about the dangers of underage drinking," Sen. Chuck Hagel of Nebraska, a cosponsor and Republican, said in a statement after the bill's reintroduction in February [2005].

One section would provide $1 million a year to craft a media campaign targeting adults that might serve as a national model.

"We need help in getting the point across," Hackett said. "There is so much persuasive [competing] media encouraging [people] to drink."

In addition, the Drug-Free Communities program would get $5 million, and $5 million more would finance efforts to create coalitions to combat underage drinking and alcohol abuse among college students.

Wendy J. Hamilton, president of MADD, supports the legislation, but says efforts should not end there.

"The money being asked for is really, in the big scheme of things, quite small—it's only about $19 million," said Hamilton, whose sister and nephew died in a drunk driving accident. "We believe much more money has to be put in, [but] this gets the ball rolling."

Another piece of pending federal legislation aims to curb underage drinking by revoking the driver's licenses of adults who provide alcohol to teens.

Similar bills, holding adults responsible for underage drinking, have gained popularity in statehouses across the country. Thirty-five states have passed some type of "social host" legislation in the past decade.

## Educating Teens About Alcohol

Everyone—especially young people—needs to be educated on the subject, especially the dangers of alcohol, said Zailckas, who drank excessively for nine years.

"There is a real lack of complete alcoholic education in school outside of drinking and driving education," she said. "I really think, at this point in time, it does have to be all of us who deal with that as [a] culture," Zailckas added. "It has to be students and parents and administrations and the government."

*"Binge drinking among young people is clearly declining and it has been doing so for many years."*

# Binge Drinking Is Declining Among Youths

## David J. Hanson

*In the following viewpoint David J. Hanson argues that media coverage of binge drinking among youths exaggerates the problem and erroneously suggests that binge drinking is increasing, rather than decreasing. He asserts that many antidrug organizations define binge drinking too broadly—as having four glasses of wine over the course of an evening, say—in order to make alcohol abuse among youths seem a more serious problem than it really is. Hanson's position is that binge drinking is actually declining and that alcohol abstinence is increasing among youths. Hanson, professor emeritus of sociology at the State University of New York at Potsdam, has spent more than three decades studying alcohol and collegiate drinking and serving as a policy and research consultant throughout North America.*

As you read, consider the following questions:

David J. Hanson, "Binge Drinking," in *Alcohol Problems and Solutions*, 2004.

1. How does Hanson contrast traditional definitions of binge drinking with standards set by some contemporary American researchers?

2. Upon what evidence does Hanson base his viewpoint that binge drinking is declining among college students in the United States?

3. According to the author, why is it dangerous for young people to believe media assertions that binge drinking is on the rise?

To most people, binge drinking brings to mind a self-destructive and unrestrained drinking bout lasting for at least a couple of days during which time the heavily intoxicated drinker "drops out" by not working, ignoring responsibilities, squandering money, and engaging in other harmful behaviors such as fighting or risky sex. This view is consistent with that portrayed in dictionary definitions, in literature, in art, and in plays or films such as the classic *Come Back Little Sheba* and *Lost Weekend* or the [more] recent *Leaving Las Vegas* [1995].

It is also consistent with the usage of physicians and other clinicians. As the editor of the *Journal of Studies on Alcohol* emphasizes, *binge* describes an extended period of time (typically at least two days) during which time a person repeatedly becomes intoxicated and gives up his or her usual activities and obligations in order to become intoxicated. It is the combination of prolonged use and the giving up of usual activities that forms the core of the clinical definition of *binge*.

Other researchers have explained that it is counter-productive to brand as pathological the consumption of only five drinks over the course of an evening of eating and social-izing. It is clearly inappropriate to equate it with a binge.

## Drinking in Other Countries

A recent Swedish study, for example, defines a binge as the consumption of half a bottle of spirits or two bottles of wine on the same occasion. Similarly, a study in Italy found that consuming an average of eight drinks a day was considered normal drinking—clearly not bingeing. In the United Kingdom, bingeing is commonly defined as consuming 11 or more drinks on an occasion. But in the United States, some researchers have defined bingeing as consuming five or more drinks on an occasion (an "occasion" can refer to an entire day). And now some have even expanded the definition to include consuming four or more drinks on an occasion by a woman.

Consider a woman who has two glasses of wine with her leisurely dinner and then sips two more drinks over the course of a four or five hour evening. In the view of most people, such a woman would be acting responsibly. Indeed her blood alcohol content would remain low. It's difficult to imagine that she would even be able to feel the effects of the alcohol. However, some researchers would now define her as a binger!

How useful is such an unrealistic definition? It is very useful if the intent is to inflate the extent of a social problem. And it would please members of the Prohibition Party and the Women's Christian Temperance Union. But it is not very useful if the intent is to accurately describe reality to the average person.

It is highly unrealistic and inappropriate to apply a prohibitionist definition to describe drinking in the United States today. Perhaps we should define binge drinking as any intoxicated drinking that leads to certain harmful or destructive behaviors. Perhaps we should at least require that a person have a certain minimum level of alcohol in the bloodstream as a prerequisite to be considered a binger. Perhaps we could even require that a person be intoxicated before being labeled a "binger." But one thing is certain: the unrealistic definitions being promoted by some researchers are misleading and deceptive at best.

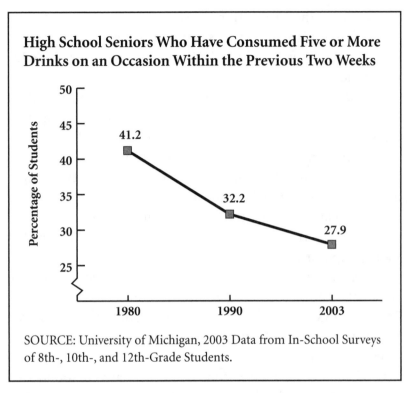

**High School Seniors Who Have Consumed Five or More Drinks on an Occasion Within the Previous Two Weeks**

SOURCE: University of Michigan, 2003 Data from In-School Surveys of 8th-, 10th-, and 12th-Grade Students.

The conclusion is clear: Be very skeptical the next time you hear or read a report about "binge" drinking. Were the people in question really bingeing? By any reasonable definition, most almost certainly were not.

## The Extent of Binge Drinking

While a continuing barrage of newspaper articles, TV shows, and special interest group reports claim that binge drinking among young people is a growing epidemic, the actual fact is quite to the contrary. Binge drinking among young people is clearly declining and it has been doing so for many years.

[According to data collected in 2003 by University of Michigan researchers,] "binge" drinking among high school seniors has declined from 41.2% to 27.9% between 1980 and 2003. That's a drop of almost one-third (32.3%).

Similarly, the proportion of U.S. military personnel who "binge" has also declined significantly, according to six worldwide surveys conducted for the military over a ... 15-year period.

"Binge" drinking is also down among American college students, and it has clearly been declining for a number of years. This is clear.

For example, according to a recent study of college drinking by Dr. Henry Wechsler of Harvard University, "binge" drinking has decreased significantly across the country over the four years since his earlier study. His research also found that the proportion of abstainers jumped nearly 22% in that short period of time.

These findings are consistent with data collected for the National Institute on Drug Abuse by the Institute for Social Research (ISR) at the University of Michigan. The ISR research found that college "binge" drinking in the United States recently reached the lowest level of the entire 17-year period that its surveys have been conducted. Similarly, it found that the proportion of drinkers has reached an all-time low among college students.

Research conducted at colleges across the United States repeatedly since the early 1980s by Drs. David Hanson (State University of New York) and Ruth Engs (Indiana University) has found declines over that time both in the proportion of collegians who drink at a high level and in the proportion who drink any alcohol.

So the facts are clear. *"Binge" drinking is down and abstinence is up among American college students. Yet in spite of this and other overwhelming evidence, the false impression persists that drinking is increasing and that "bingeing continues unabated."*

## So What's the Harm?

This misperception is dangerous because when young people go off to college falsely thinking that "everybody" is drinking and bingeing, they are more likely to drink and to "binge" in order to conform. Correcting this misperception is important because it can empower young people and break the vicious self-fulfilling prophecy that helps perpetuate collegiate alcohol abuse.

Individual students almost always believe that most others on campus drink more heavily than they do and the disparity between the perceived and the actual behaviors tends to be quite large. By conducting surveys of actual student behavior and publicizing the results, the extent of heavy drinking can be quickly and significantly reduced. The most carefully assessed such abuse prevention project on campus has demonstrated a 35% reduction in heavy drinking, a 31% reduction in alcohol-related injuries to self, and a 54% reduction in alcohol-related injuries to others. And similar results have been demonstrated at colleges across the country with this quick and inexpensive approach.

Too many college students still abuse alcohol. But people who exaggerate the problem and distort its magnitude are actually making the problem worse. If we are to further reduce alcohol abuse and the problems it causes, we have to publicize the actual facts and correct damaging misperceptions. Doing so will empower students to do what they as individuals generally want to do: drink less or not drink at all.

The challenge of correcting dangerous misperceptions about college student drinking is enormous. Many researchers and others have a vested interest in inflating the extent of "binge" drinking and stories of drinking epidemics make dramatic headlines that sell more publications. But scare tactics are actually counter-productive and it turns out that *the most effective way to reduce alcohol abuse is simply to tell the truth and make sure that young people understand the facts.*

> "People who used marijuana are 8 times more likely to have used cocaine, 15 times more likely to have used heroin, and 5 times more likely to develop a need for treatment."

# Teen Marijuana Use Is a Serious Threat

*Scott Burns*

*Scott Burns is the deputy director for state and local affairs at the Office of National Drug Control Policy, a White House agency established to reduce drug use. In the following viewpoint he asserts that marijuana poses a threat to youths more than any other illicit drug. Burns argues that marijuana is a gateway drug that leads to use of cocaine and heroin, and that it is addictive and linked to violence in youth. He further contends that efforts to normalize and legalize the use of marijuana for any purpose are misguided and dangerous.*

As you read, consider the following questions:

1. How does Burns support his claim that marijuana is linked to violence?

Scott Burns, "An Open Letter to America's Prosecutors," Office of National Drug Control Policy, 2002.

2. What are the statistical relationships between cocaine and marijuana, and between heroin and marijuana, according to the author?

3. According to the author, what medical "benefits" are associated with the chemicals in marijuana?

There is a serious drug problem in this country. As the former Iron County, Utah prosecuting attorney, I know that prosecutors see the problem every day in the courtroom, on the street, and in neighborhoods. Meanwhile, this country is faced with a subtle but powerful threat to exacerbate the problem: well-financed and deceptive campaigns to normalize and ultimately legalize the use of marijuana.

This is important, because nationwide, *no drug matches the threat posed by marijuana*. It is a much bigger problem than most people, including some in law enforcement, realize. Out of 16 million drug users in America, about 77% use marijuana, and 60% of teenagers in treatment have a *primary* marijuana diagnosis.

This means that the addiction to marijuana by our youth exceeds their addiction rates for alcohol, cocaine, heroin, methamphetamine, ecstasy and all other illegal drugs *combined*. And the initiation rate for marijuana looks to be getting younger.

Drug policy "reformers" say that our anti-drug efforts, especially those of prosecutors and police, are doomed to fail. This is absolutely false. We may never rid this country of every crack pipe or marijuana plant. However, research proves that we have made substantial success in reducing drug use in this country before, and with your help, we are doing it again.

One of the best ways to make a difference is for local leaders . . . to take a stand publicly and tell Americans the truth.

The *truth* is that *marijuana is not harmless*. As a factor in emergency room visits, marijuana has risen 176% since 1994, and now surpasses heroin. Smoking marijuana leads to changes in the brain similar to those caused by the use of cocaine and heroin, and affects alertness, concentration, perception, coordination, and reaction time. One recent study involving a roadside check of reckless drivers (not impaired by alcohol) showed that 45% tested positive for marijuana.

The *truth* is that *marijuana is addictive.* Average THC [tetrahydrocannabinol—marijuana's active ingredient] levels rose from less than 1% in the late 1970s to more than 7% in 2001, and sinsemilla potency increased from 6% to 13%, and now reaches as high as 33%. Marijuana users have an addiction rate of about 10%, and of the 5.6 million drug users who are suffering from illegal drug dependence or abuse, 62% are dependent on or are abusing marijuana.

The *truth* is that *marijuana and violence are linked.* Research shows a link between frequent marijuana use and increased violent behavior, and youth who use marijuana weekly are nearly four times more likely than non-users to engage in violence.

The *truth* is that *"we aren't imprisoning"* individuals for just *"smoking a joint."* Overwhelmingly, we treat drug users, and especially marijuana users. Nationwide, the percentage of those in prison for marijuana possession as their most serious offense is less than half of one percent (0.46%), and those generally involved exceptional circumstances.

The *truth* is that *marijuana is a gateway drug* for many people. Not every person that uses marijuana will go on to use other drugs, but the overwhelming majority of people using other dangerous drugs—about 99%—began by smoking "a little weed." People who used marijuana are 8 times more likely to have used cocaine, 15 times more likely to have used heroin, and 5 times more likely to develop a need for treatment of abuse or dependence on ANY drug.

The *truth* is that *marijuana legalization would be a nightmare* in America. After Dutch coffee shops started selling

## Marijuana Use Among Teens

Marijuana is the most widely used illicit drug used by teens today. Approximately 60 percent of the kids who use drugs use only marijuana. Of the 14.6 million marijuana users in 2002, approximately 4.8 million used it on 20 or more days in any given month.

The marijuana that is available to teens today is much stronger than the marijuana that was available in the 1960's. Sometimes it is also laced with other, more potent drugs. Marijuana is physically addictive. Each year, 100,000 teens are treated for marijuana dependence. Teens who smoke marijuana heavily experience much the same symptoms of withdrawal as users of nicotine . . . .

Kids are using marijuana at an earlier age. Research indicates that the earlier teens start using marijuana, the more likely they are to become dependent on this or other drugs later in life. Of teens admitted for treatment for marijuana dependence, 56 percent had first used the drug by fourteen years of age, and 26 percent had begun by twelve years of age.

*Teen Help LLC,* Teen Drug Abuse, *2004.*

marijuana in small quantities, use of the drug nearly tripled (from 15 percent to 44 percent) among 18–20 year olds between 1984 and 1996. While our nation's cocaine consumption has decreased by 80 percent over the past 15 years, Europe's has increased . . . and the Dutch government has started to reconsider its policies.

The *truth* is that *marijuana is not a medicine,* and no credible research suggests that it is. There is a protocol to allow some drugs—like cocaine and methamphetamine—to be prescribed in limited cases. Our medical system is the best in the world, and it relies on proven scientific research, not opinions or anecdotes. The primary medical "benefit" of the numerous chemicals in marijuana are increased risk of cancer, lung damage, and poor pregnancy outcomes.

> *"Of all people who have tried marijuana, less than one third will try cocaine or hallucinogens, and less than four percent of marijuana smokers will try heroin."*

# Teen Marijuana Use Is Not a Serious Threat

*Brian C. Bennett*

*In the following viewpoint Brian C. Bennett argues that marijuana is not a gateway drug that leads to the use of more dangerous drugs. Bennett uses the statistics published by the National Office of Drug Control Policy to refute the federal government's claim that marijuana use leads to the use of other drugs. According to Bennett's interpretation of government data, if marijuana is truly a gateway drug, many more people would be using drugs such as cocaine or heroin than are actually doing so. Instead, maintains Bennett, the majority of people who use marijuana never use any other drug. Bennett is a freelance writer and antidrug-war activist.*

As you read, consider the following questions:

Brian C. Bennett, "Assessing the Marijuana 'Gateway' Theory," *BBSNews*, January 15, 2003. Reproduced by permission.

1. According to Bennett, what is the best way to assess the gateway theory of marijuana use?

2. Bennett notes that across the population there is a wide variance in risk tolerance; how is this relevant to the relationship between marijuana and drugs like cocaine and heroin, in his opinion?

3. How many people will use cocaine after smoking marijuana, according to the author?

The Office of National Drug Control Policy (ONDCP) tells us that "marijuana users are 8 times more likely to have used cocaine, 15 times more likely to have used heroin, and 5 times more likely to develop a need for treatment of abuse or dependence on ANY drug." These statistics, according to the ONDCP, prove that marijuana is a gateway to the use of other drugs. Before we give in to the hysteria and hand wringing though, let's have a look at what's really going on.

The National Household Survey on Drug Abuse (NHSDA) is an annual survey produced under the auspices of the U.S. Department of Health and Human Services, and serves as the basis for many of the claims made by ONDCP concerning drug use in America.

If we take the time to look at the data from this survey, however, we can quickly see that ONDCP is, shall we say, grossly distorting and exaggerating the "threat" posed to our society by marijuana use.

## Looking for Patterns

In order to determine the likelihood that using one drug will lead to the use of another, it would be helpful to have some idea of exactly how many people have used various drugs. If we have those numbers we can better make comparisons and determinations about patterns of drug use. Fortunately, the NHSDA gives us exactly the data we need.

from them, and hardly any of them feel compelled to walk about on the outside of them or chuck a parachute out then jump after it.

What is actually going on is something much simpler: people have different toleration of, and requirements for, taking risks. Those who will engage in a high risk behavior are naturally more likely to engage in lower risk behaviors. So, as sure as the ONDCP declares, "99 percent of those who use other drugs will have begun by smoking a little weed." Just as 99 percent of those who jump out of airplanes probably started out by riding in them first.

When it comes to marijuana and the use of other drugs, the more proper description of the relationships is this: Of all people who have tried marijuana, less than one third will try cocaine or hallucinogens, and less than four percent of marijuana smokers will try heroin.

As former drug "czar" Barry McCaffrey was fond of saying "you're entitled to your own opinion, but you're not entitled to your own data." That's why I use his data.

> "Pharming parties—or just
> 'pharming'—represent a growing trend
> among teenage drug abusers."

# Teens Are Abusing
# Prescription Drugs

## Carolyn Banta

*In the following viewpoint Carolyn Banta asserts that prescription drug abuse is emerging as a serious threat to teens. She reports on "pharming" parties at which teens barter and trade prescription drugs for recreational use. The abuse of these drugs—including painkillers such as OxyContin and Vicodin, and antianxiety medicines such as Xanax—has been called the next epidemic in teen drug abuse and addiction. At the time of this writing, Banta, then a senior at Lehigh University pursuing a double major in science writing and science, technology, and society, was an editorial intern at* Time *magazine.*

As you read, consider the following questions:

1. According to Banta, how do teens typically acquire supplies of prescription drugs?

2. What circumstances lead teens to treat the use of prescription drugs casually, according to Banta?

3. According to the author, what is the relationship between prescription drug abuse and the use of other substances, including alcohol?

In the basement of a Cape Cod on a suburban street in northern New Jersey, a teenage boy turns to a friend and asks impatiently, "What did you get? I'll give you some of this"—indicating a bottle of Ritalin stuffed into the front pocket of his backpack—"for some of that painkiller." As a rap song plays just loud enough not to disturb the neighbors, his friend eyes the bottle suspiciously. "Is this generic, or is it the good stuff?" he asks. Upstairs, several teens are sitting at the kitchen table listening to a girl who looks to be about 15 tell how she got the narcotic Oxycontin from the medicine cabinet at home. "It was left over," she says, "from my sister's wisdom-teeth surgery."

This isn't an ordinary party—it's a pharming party, a get-together arranged while parents are out so the kids can barter for their favorite prescription drugs. Pharming parties—or just "pharming" (from pharmaceuticals)—represent a growing trend among teenage drug abusers. While use of illegal substances like speed, heroin and pot has declined over the past decade, according to a report issued three weeks ago by Columbia University's National Center on Addiction and Substance Abuse (CASA), abuse of prescription drugs has increased sharply. CASA says about 2.3 million kids ages 12 to 17 took legal medications illegally in 2003, the latest year for which figures are available. That's three times the number in 1992, or about 1 out of every 10 teens. "It's a hidden epidemic," says Dr. Nicholas Pace, an internist at New York University Medical Center. "Parents don't want to admit there's a problem out there."

The problem isn't just that kids can easily become addicted to painkillers like Oxycontin or Vicodin, antianxiety

## A Short History of OxyContin Abuse

In 1999, approximately 221,000 people age twelve or over had used OxyContin without a prescription. In 2000, that figure jumped to 399,000, and in 2001 it more than doubled again to 957,000 people. In 2002, researchers reported that more than four hundred deaths have been linked to Oxy-Contin.

*Katherine Ketcham and Nicholas A. Pace,*
Teens Under the Influence, *2003.*

medicines like Valium or Xanax, or attention-deficit-disorder drugs like Ritalin and Adderall. Taken without proper supervision, those medicines can send kids to the emergency room. They can lead to difficulty breathing, a drop or rapid increase in heart rate or trouble responding when driving a car, especially when the drugs are combined with alcohol, as they often are. Pain medications, which are also powerful nervous-system depressants, are particularly dangerous—and especially prized. "If I have something good, like Oxycontin, it might be worth two or three Xanax," says a 17-year-old pharming veteran who was one of more than a dozen guests (and one of the few girls) at the New Jersey party. "We rejoice when someone has a medical thing, like, gets their wisdom teeth out or has back pain, because we know we'll get pills. Last year I had gum surgery, and I thought, Well, at least I'll get painkillers."

Unfortunately, prescription drugs are often far easier to obtain than illegal ones. Some teenagers come by their pills legitimately but trade them for others, like painkillers, that hold more appeal because of their more potent high. Others order from shady Internet pharmacies where prescriptions aren't always required. Still others take advantage of the fact that neither doctors nor parents tend to think of prescription medications as drugs of abuse. That makes it a fairly easy proposition to fake or exaggerate symptoms in order to persuade physicians to write prescriptions, or to pillage medicine cabinets for pills left forgotten on shelves. "When adults and medical professionals treat medications casually," says Dr. Francis Hayden, director of the adolescent mental-health center at Mount Sinai Hospital in New York City, "we need not be surprised that adolescents are treating them casually."

Worse yet, many of these kids are abusing illegal drugs at the same time. According to the CASA report, about 75% of prescription-drug abusers are so-called polysubstance users who also take other drugs or drink—most of the New Jersey kids, for instance, were downing their pills with Miller Lite. "My friend told me to save the painkillers for when I'm drinking or getting high," says the 17-year-old with a chuckle as she smokes her last cigarette and flings the empty pack into the backyard. She doesn't think of herself as an addict. But she recognizes the signs of addiction among her friends. "I know a lot of people who live by pills," she says. "They take a pill to wake them up, another pill to put them to sleep, one to make them hungry and another to stop the hunger. Pills can dictate your life—I've seen it."

| "Inhalant abuse reaches its peak at some point during the seventh through ninth grades."

# Teen Inhalant Abuse Is a Serious Problem

**National Institute on Drug Abuse**

*The National Institute on Drug Abuse (NIDA) is an agency of the federal government that conducts research in an effort to prevent drug abuse and addiction. In the following viewpoint NIDA outlines the problem of inhalant abuse in the United States, noting that these toxic substances are primarily abused by young people. NIDA reports that inhalant use among teenagers has decreased since its peak in 1995. However, it remains unacceptably high overall, and in recent years it has increased among eighth-graders. Inhalant abuse can have devastating consequences, according to NIDA, including convulsions, coma, and even death.*

As you read, consider the following questions:

1. What are the four types of inhalants, as defined by NIDA?

*Research Report Series*, Bethesda, MD: National Institute on Drug Abuse, 2005. Reproduced by permission.

2. As reported by NIDA, what percentage of eighth-graders reported lifetime use of inhalants in 2004?

3. What is "sudden sniffing death," as described by NIDA?

Inhalants are volatile substances that produce chemical vapors that can be inhaled to induce a psychoactive, or mind-altering, effect. Although other abused substances can be inhaled, the term "inhalants" is used to describe a variety of substances whose main common characteristic is that they are rarely, if ever, taken by any route other than inhalation. This definition encompasses a broad range of chemicals found in hundreds of different products that may have different pharmacological effects. As a result, precise categorization of inhalants is difficult. One clarification system lists four general categories of inhalants—volatile solvents, aerosols, gases, and nitrites—based on the form in which they are often found in household, industrial, and medical products.

## Types of Inhalants

*Volatile solvents* are liquids that vaporize at room temperatures. They are found in a multitude of inexpensive, easily available products used for common household and industrial purposes. These include paint thinners and removers, dry-cleaning fluids, degreasers, gasoline, glues, correction fluids, and felt-tip marker fluids.

*Aerosols* are sprays that contain propellants and solvents. They include spray paints, deodorant and hair sprays, vegetable oil sprays for cooking, and fabric protector sprays.

*Gases* include medical anesthetics as well as gases used in household or commercial products. Medical anesthetic gases include ether, chloroform, halothane, and nitrous oxide, commonly called "laughing gas." Nitrous oxide is the most abused of these gases and can be found in whipped cream dispensers and products that boost octane levels in racing cars.

Household or commercial products containing gases include butane lighters, propane tanks, whipped cream dispensers, and refrigerants.

*Nitrites* often are considered a special class of inhalants. Unlike most other inhalants, which act directly on the central nervous system (CNS), nitrites act primarily to dilate blood vessels and relax the muscles. While other inhalants are used to alter mood, nitrites are used primarily as sexual enhancers. Nitrites include cyclohexyl nitrite, isoamyl (amyl) nitrite, and isobutyl (butyl) nitrite, and are commonly known as "poppers" or "snappers." Amyl nitrite is used in certain diagnostic procedures and was prescribed in the past to treat some patients for heart pain. Nitrites are now prohibited by the Consumer Product Safety Commission, but can still be found, sold in small bottles, often labeled as "video head cleaner," "room deodorizer," "leather cleaner," or "liquid aroma."

## Patterns of Inhalant Abuse

Inhalants—particularly volatile solvents, gases, and aerosols—are often among the first drugs that young children use. One national survey indicates that about 3.0 percent of U.S. children have tried inhalants by the time they reach fourth grade. Inhalant abuse can become chronic and extend into adulthood.

Generally, inhalant abusers will abuse any available substance. However, effects produced by individual inhalants vary, and some individuals will go out of their way to obtain their favorite inhalant. For example, in certain parts of the country, "Texas shoe-shine," a shoe-shining spray containing the chemical toluene, is a local favorite. Silver and gold spray paints, which contain more toluene than other spray colors, also are popular inhalants.

Data from national and State surveys suggest inhalant abuse reaches its peak at some point during the seventh through ninth grades. In the Monitoring the Future (MTF) study, an annual NIDA-supported survey of the Nation's secondary school students, 8th-graders also regularly report the highest rate of current, past year, and lifetime inhalant abuse; 10th- and 12th-graders report less abuse.

Gender differences in inhalant abuse have been identified at different points in childhood. The 2004 MTF indicates that 10.5 percent of 8th grade females reported using inhalants in the past year, compared with 8.8 percent of 8th grade males. Among 12th-graders, 3.4 percent of females and 4.8 percent of males reported using inhalants in the past year. The National Survey on Drug Use and Health (NSDUH), an annual survey of drug use among the Nation's noninstitutionalized civilians, reports that similar percentages of 12- to 17-year-old boys and girls abused inhalants in 2003. However, the percentage of 18- to 25-year-old males who abused inhalants within the past month was more than twice that of females in that age group, suggesting that sustained abuse of inhalants is more common among males.

People who abuse inhalants are found in both urban and rural settings. Research on factors contributing to inhalant abuse suggests that adverse socioeconomic conditions, a history of childhood abuse, poor grades, and dropping out of school all are associated with inhalant abuse.

## The Scope of Inhalant Abuse

Inhalant abuse was up significantly for the second year in a row among 8th-graders, according to the latest MTF data, while use among 10th- and 12th-graders continued to decline.

- The rate of high school seniors who abused inhalants in the past year was 4.2 percent in 2004, down from the peak of 8.0 percent in 1995.

- Annual abuse of inhalants among 10th-graders was 5.9 percent in 2004, also down from a high in 1995 (9.6 percent).

- Among 8th-graders, 2004 abuse figures, at 9.6 percent,

were down overall from the 1995 peak of 12.8 percent, but were up from the 2002 rate of 7.7 percent.

According to the 2003 NSDUH, lifetime, past year, and past month inhalant use among persons aged 12 to 17 were 10.7 percent, 4.5 percent, and 1.3 percent, respectively. The number of new inhalant users increased from 627,000 new users in 1994 to 1 million in 2002. Inhalant initiates were predominantly under age 18 (78 percent in 2002).

MTF's lifetime prevalence figures indicate that the percentages of students who have tried inhalants continue to decrease steadily for 10th- and 12th-graders. In 2004, 12.4 percent of 10th-graders and 11.9 percent of 12th-graders said they have abused inhalants at least once in their lives. Although lifetime prevalence peaked for 8th-graders in 1995 (21.6 percent), rates of inhalant use among this group are still high. In fact, 8th-graders reported a significant increase in lifetime use from 15.8 percent in 2003 to 17.3 percent in 2004. For 10th-graders, the peak was 19.3 percent in 1996. For seniors, rates were highest in 1994 at 17.7 percent. These data raise a question: How can fewer 12th-graders than 8th-graders consistently report they have ever abused inhalants? Possibly, many 12th-graders fail to recall their much earlier use of inhalants or, more troubling, many 8th-grade inhalant abusers may have dropped out of school by the 12th grade and are no longer included in the survey population . . . .

## Effects of Inhalant Use

Although the chemical substances found in inhalants may produce various pharmacological effects, most inhalants produce a rapid high that resembles alcohol intoxication with initial excitation, then drowsiness, disinhibition, light-headedness, and agitation. If sufficient amounts are inhaled, nearly all solvents and gases produce anesthesia, a loss of sensation, and even unconsciousness.

The chemicals found in solvents, aerosol sprays, and gases can produce a variety of additional effects during or shortly after use. These effects are related to inhalant intoxication and may include belligerence, apathy, impaired judgment, and impaired functioning in work or social situations. Dizziness, drowsiness, slurred speech, lethargy, depressed reflexes, general muscle weakness, and stupor are other possible effects. For example, research shows that toluene can produce headache, euphoria, giddy feelings, and inability to coordinate movements. Exposure to high doses can cause confusion and delirium. Nausea and vomiting are other common side effects.

Inhaled nitrites dilate blood vessels, increase heart rate, and produce a sensation of heat and excitement that can last for several minutes. Other effects can include flush, dizziness, and headache. Unlike other inhalants, which are abused mainly for their intoxicating effects, nitrites are abused primarily because they are believed to enhance sexual pleasure and performance.

A strong need to continue using inhalants has been reported among many individuals, particularly those who abuse inhalants for prolonged periods over many days. Compulsive use and a mild withdrawal syndrome can occur with long-term inhalant abuse. Additional symptoms exhibited by long-term inhalant abusers include weight loss, muscle weakness, disorientation, inattentiveness, lack of coordination, irritability, and depression.

## The Medical Consequences

Inhalant abusers risk an array of devastating medical consequences. Prolonged sniffing of the highly concentrated chemicals in solvents or aerosol sprays can induce irregular and rapid heart rhythms and lead to heart failure and death within minutes of a session of prolonged sniffing. This syndrome, known as "sudden sniffing death," can result from a single session of inhalant use by an otherwise healthy young person. Sudden sniffing death is particularly associated with the abuse of butane, propane, and chemicals in aerosols. Inhalant abuse also can cause death by:

- Asphyxiation—from repeated inhalations, which lead to high concentrations of inhaled fumes displacing the available oxygen in the lungs;

- Suffocation—from blocking air from entering the lungs when inhaling fumes from a plastic bag placed over the head;

- Convulsions or seizures—caused by abnormal electrical discharges in the brain;

- Coma—the brain shuts down all but the most vital functions;

- Choking—from inhalation of vomit after inhalant use; or

- Fatal injury—from accidents, including motor vehicle fatalities, suffered while intoxicated.

Animal and human research shows that most inhalants are extremely toxic. Perhaps the most significant toxic effect of chronic exposure to inhalants is widespread and long-lasting damage to the brain and other parts of the nervous system. For example, both animal research and human pathological studies indicate that chronic abuse of volatile solvents such as toluene damages the protective sheath around certain nerve fibers in the brain and peripheral nervous system. This extensive destruction of nerve fibers is clinically similar to that seen with neurological diseases such as multiple sclerosis.

The neurotoxic effects of prolonged inhalant abuse include neurological syndromes that reflect damage to parts of the brain involved in controlling cognition, movement, vision, and hearing. Cognitive abnormalities can range from mild impairment to severe dementia. Other effects can include difficulty coordinating movement, limb spasms, and loss of feeling, hearing, and vision.

Inhalants also are highly toxic to other organs. Chronic exposure can produce significant damage to the heart, lungs, liver, and kidneys. Although some inhalant-induced damage to the nervous and other organ systems may be at least partially reversible when inhalant abuse is stopped, many syndromes caused by repeated or prolonged abuse are irreversible.

> *"Youths can buy the medicines easily, then go to Web sites to learn how much someone of their weight should take to get high."*

# Youths Are Abusing Over-the-Counter Drugs

*Donna Leinwand*

*In the following viewpoint Donna Leinwand reports on the increase in teen abuse of non-prescription cough and cold medicines. Instead of trying to get high on cough syrups, as adolescents have done in the past, Leinwand notes, today's youths are using pills and capsules containing dextromethorphan (DXM). These are inexpensive, readily available in drugstores and supermarkets, and easier to swallow than cough syrup. Leinwand points out that cough and cold medicine overdoses tend to occur in isolated outbreaks across the country, often surprising parents, educators, and law enforcement officials. In response to the threat, retailers have begun to monitor the sale of products containing DXM, writes Leinward. Donna Leinward is a reporter for USA Today.*

As you read, consider the following questions:

1. According to the author, how are drugstores and pharmaceutical companies responding to youth abuse of cold and cough medicines containing DXM?

2. Which age group is most likely to abuse DXM, as reported by Leinward?

3. What are the risks associated with DXM overdose, as reported by the author?

Emergency rooms and schools across the nation are reporting that waves of youths are overdosing on non-prescription cough and cold medicines that are widely available in drugstores and supermarkets.

The dozens of overdoses in the past two years—including at least five deaths in which the abuse of over-the-counter [OTC] medicines was a factor—reflect how medicines such as Robitussin and Coricidin are becoming more popular as recreational drugs for kids as young as 12, police and doctors say.

The incidents represent a dangerous turn from past decades, when some youths would guzzle cough syrup to try to get a buzz from alcohol and codeine, authorities say. Most cough and cold medicines no longer contain alcohol, and those with codeine, an addictive opiate, are available only by prescription. But more than 120 over-the-counter medicines include dextromethorphan, or DXM, a cough suppressant that when taken in heavy doses can produce hallucinations and a loss of motor control, much as PCP does.

Kids don't have to drink entire bottles of goopy cough syrup to go "Robotripping" or "Dexing." Pills such as Coricidin HBP Cough & Cold tablets—known as "Triple C's"—offer far more potent doses of DXM with less hassle. Youths can buy the medicines easily, then go to Web sites to learn how much someone of their weight should take to get high.

## A Cheap High

Whether in cough syrup or pills, DXM costs just a few dollars, is "easy to get . . . and there's a lot of information about how to get high on it on the Internet," says Charles Nozicka, medical director of pediatric emergency medicine at St. Alexius Medical Center in Hoffman Estates, Ill., west of Chicago. He says that he began seeing DXM overdoses among teens three or four years ago, and that lately he has seen as many as four cases a week.

Authorities say DXM overdoses typically occur in clusters, as word of the drug spreads in a community's middle schools and high schools. This fall [2003], parents and school officials in Naples, Fla., who had known little about DXM were shocked when several kids in their early teens suddenly passed out in class after overdosing on the drug.

At Pine Ridge Middle School in Naples in September, a 13-year-old girl brought about 80 Coricidin pills to campus one day and gave some to six friends, authorities there say. Each of the friends took at least five pills—the recommended dosage for adults is no more than one pill every six hours—and soon the school was in chaos. Two students lost consciousness in their first-period classes; they and one other overdosed youth were treated at a local hospital.

The girl who distributed the pills thought it would be "fun to feel messed up and act . . . drunk," says Cpl. Joseph Scott of the sheriff's office in Collier County, which is in southwestern Florida on the Gulf Coast.

Another round of overdoses occurred on Nov. 6 at Immokalee High School, which also is in Collier County. A 15-year-old girl and two of her friends took five Coricidin pills each before school. By 10:45 a.m., the girl "couldn't remember her own name," Scott says. When paramedics could not stabilize her heartbeat, they called for a helicopter to take her to a hospital. Authorities learned later that she had obtained the pills from a boy who had taken them from his home. The girl's friends did not have to be hospitalized.

Scott says that many parents in Collier County were shaken by the idea that youths could buy large amounts of such a potentially dangerous drug at a local store, and then consume the drug, without breaking any laws. "It's something people aren't really informed about yet. The parents we've dealt with so far are pretty much in shock," Scott says. "It seems right now it's mostly the younger kids" who are taking DXM.

Scott says his office is compiling information packets about DXM that will be distributed to local pharmacies and schools.

## Restricting Access

Elsewhere, growing concerns about DXM have led some drugstores to restrict access to cough and cold medicines.

After two teenage girls and two 20-year-old men in Merrill, Wis., overdosed on medicines containing DXM this year [2003], some drugstores in the city of about 10,000 people 160 miles north of Madison began to stow such remedies behind their counters. At the Aurora Pharmacy, customers now must request Coricidin tablets, and they aren't allowed to buy several boxes at once. Pharmacist Jim Becker says he wants the drug "where we can keep an eye on it."

Drug manufacturers say they sympathize with concerns about drug abuse, but they have resisted efforts to restrict consumers' access to Coricidin, Robitussin and other remedies containing DXM.

"The vast majority of people take them responsibly," says Fran Sullivan, spokesman for Wyeth Consumer Healthcare in Madison, N.J., which makes Robitussin products. "As a medicine, it works hands-down, so we want people to be able to use it if they need it."

Aware that teens might be tempted to abuse its newest DXM product, anti-cough gel-tabs, Wyeth made its packaging large enough so that it is difficult to stash in a backpack or pocket, Sullivan says. The company advertises on TV shows geared to adults, he says.

"We've noticed that the abuse comes and goes in waves," he says. "It gets really popular in a small area for a short period of time and then it dies out. Teens end up in the emergency room, it makes the local newspaper, and the area goes on alert."

Schering-Plough, which makes Coricidin, is working with the Partnership for a Drug-Free America to create an educational Web site on DXM, company spokeswoman Mary-Fran Faraji says. Company representatives also are meeting with pharmacists, parents, schools and retailers to discuss ways to prevent drug abuse.

But Faraji says Schering-Plough doesn't plan to eliminate DXM from its non-prescription cough and cold medicines. She notes that most of the potential alternatives to DXM as a cough suppressant are opiates that carry more potential for abuse. "Reformulating our product is not going to make the abuse issue go away," Faraji says. "Our product is safe and effective when used as directed."

## DXM Approved Decades Ago

DXM, a synthetic drug that chemically is similar to morphine, was approved by the Food and Drug Administration as a cough suppressant in 1954. Drug manufacturers began putting it in cough syrups in the 1970s as a replacement for codeine.

DXM is sold legally without a prescription because it does not make users high when taken in small doses. The recommended dose, about one-sixth to one-third of an ounce of an extra-strength cough syrup, contains 15 to 30 milligrams of DXM, according to the National Institute on Drug Abuse. At doses of 4 or more ounces of cough syrup, DXM produces effects similar to those of PCP or the anesthetic ketamine, the institute says. DXM can produce hallucinations, depressed

## Legal, but Dangerous

They're candy coated, and the kids call them "Skittles," "Triple-C's," and "Dex." . . .

They're perfectly legal—nothing more than Coricidin Cough & Cold tablets available at any drugstore. . . .

Over the past several years, drug counselors around the country have noticed a significant hike in the abuse of the cough suppressant dextromethorphan (DXM). Poison-control centers have also reported a doubling of the number of calls since 2001. But because it's a legal drug, it's not tracked by any of the major groups that follow teen drug use. So it's difficult to gauge how just how widespread the problem is.

*Alexandra Marks,* Christian Science Monitor,
*June, 1, 2004.*

breathing, elevated blood pressure and an irregular heartbeat. Overdoses can cause seizures, comas and death.

It can be particularly dangerous when taken with other drugs.

Lee Cantrell, interim director of the California Poison Control System's San Diego division, says that Robitussin and some other cough and cold remedies containing DXM have additional ingredients that can be fatal to abusers if taken in huge doses. For example, antihistamines, which often are combined with DXM in cough and cold remedies, can be toxic and cause respiratory distress, Cantrell says. He says cough medicine abuse emerged as a problem in California about three years ago [in 2000].

During what officials called a "mini-outbreak" of DXM overdoses in New Jersey two months ago [October 2003], a

15-year-old boy had to be treated for acetaminophen poisoning after he drank two bottles of Robitussin and took some Coricidin. Acetaminophen is a pain reliever/fever reducer that, over time, can cause liver damage if taken in large doses.

The federal government does not keep statistics on DXM abuse, but drug specialists say anecdotal evidence suggests that its use does not approach that of methamphetamine or the club drug Ecstasy. DXM abusers, drug specialists say, typically are young teens who are seeking a cheap alternative to drugs that are more expensive and more difficult to get.

Still, "what we see in the emergency department is probably the tip of the iceberg," Nozicka says of DXM abuse in his community near Chicago. "There's probably a lot more going on, but most (overdose cases) don't end up in the emergency room."

Some drug counselors and doctors say young adults have begun using DXM with alcohol, Ecstasy and other drugs.

DXM "looks innocuous enough, but if you take enough of it, it can cause serious problems," says Ed Bottei, medical director of the Iowa Statewide Poison Control Center in Sioux City. A 22-year-old college student in Ames, Iowa, died of a DXM overdose in October 2002. "Even though it's an over-the-counter medicine, it can still hurt you," Bottei says.

## Tracking OTC Drug Abuse

Authorities who have been more focused on illegal drugs often have been surprised by sudden outbreaks of DXM overdoses.

After a series of overdoses in the Detroit area in August [2003], the U.S. Drug Enforcement Administration [DEA] issued an alert that warned parents, schools and local communities about an "escalation" in DXM abuse.

The alert cited a "disturbing increase" of overdoses in the Grosse Point area, near Detroit.

DEA special agent David Jacobson, spokesman for the agency's Detroit office, says that federal drug enforcement analysts usually can forecast regional trends in drug use, based on geographic patterns. But "Robotripping" came out of nowhere, he says.

"Law enforcement hadn't heard about it, but all the kids had," Jacobson says. As he and others in the community asked around, they found that DXM abuse "was not only out there, but it was out there more than we thought."

## Internet Fuels Trend

Like others who monitor DXM abuse, Jacobson says the Internet has fueled the trend.

"Now (DXM cases) pop up everywhere," he says. "If one kid is doing it anywhere, kids here will know about it."

At Michigan State University in East Lansing, the student health center is planning to include a question about DXM abuse on its next student health survey in the spring, says Dennis Martell, the university's interim coordinator for health education.

"We want to be proactive in identifying the problem before it becomes the rage," he says.

Meanwhile, as word of DXM spreads among teens and young adults, pharmacies are reporting more thefts of cough and cold medicines, as well as suspicious purchases.

Victor Vercammen, a pharmacist who works in a drugstore north of Chicago, says he recently watched two young men try to buy six packages of Coricidin. As the clerk rang up the purchase, Vercammen confronted the pair.

"I could tell as the conversation went on that they planned to misuse it, so I asked if they realized that it could cause a seizure, that it could be fatal," says Vercammen, a spokesman for the Illinois Pharmacists Association. "My hope was that educating them at least gets them to think about it. The popular conception is that because it's over-the-counter, it's safer."

The men left the packages on the counter and walked out.

# Periodical Bibliography

The following articles have been selected to supplement the diverse views presented in this chapter.

Robert Finn          "Easy Availability Driving Dextromethorphan Abuse," *Pediatric News*, May 2004.

Mary L. Gavin        "Cough and Cold Medicine Abuse," *KidsHealth for Parents*, February 2, 2004.

Amy Harmon           "Young, Assured, and Playing Pharmacist to Friends," *New York Times*, November 16, 2005.

Timothy F. Kirn      "Adolescent Use of Drugs, Tobacco Continues Decline: More Are Abusing Painkillers, Inhalants," *Clinical Psychiatry News*, February 2005.

Alexandra Marks      "Teens Use 'Legal' Cold Medicine to Get High," *Christian Science Monitor*, June 1, 2004.

Leah Paulos          "Life in a Bottle: Jordan Young Loved to Party, Until a Friend's Frightening Encounter with Alcohol Finally Sobered Her Up," *Scholastic Choices*, October 2005.

Michelle Lee Ribeiro "When Prescription Drugs Kill: Lots of People
and Sarah Richards   Think Legal Drugs Can Give You a 'Safe' High," *CosmoGirl!*, March 2005.

Nora D. Volkow       "Inhalants: A Looming Threat for All Teens," *Scholastic Choices*, November/December 2005.

**OPPOSING
VIEWPOINTS®
SERIES**

# CHAPTER 2

# What Causes Teen Drug Abuse?

# Chapter Preface

Many schools have developed zero tolerance policies in regards to the use of alcohol, tobacco, marijuana, and other controlled substances. Under this approach, any use of an illegal drug or misuse of a legal substance is considered abuse. Violating a school's zero tolerance policy may require a teen to enroll in mandatory in-patient or out-patient treatment for drug addiction. Even a first offense can lead to exclusion from sports or suspension from academic programs. Proponents say that zero tolerance policies are the only sure way to protect teens from the dangers of substance abuse. However, many experts disagree with this assessment. They contend that in fact zero tolerance policies lead to higher levels of substance abuse and increase the harmful consequences of normal teen behavior. The policy of zero tolerance is one of many factors purported to contribute to teen drug abuse.

Three primary arguments are used in support of zero tolerance policies. One is that the experimental use of alcohol and other substances leads to drug dependence and the use of more dangerous substances; therefore, no level of use or experimentation is safe. Another argument is that the threat of severe consequences will serve as a deterrent to the majority of teens, who, in order to avoid punishment, will choose not to drink, smoke, or experiment with illegal substances. The third argument is that those who are undeterred by the mere existence of the policy will be persuaded by the example of seeing peers excluded from sports, expelled from school, or enrolled in drug abuse treatment programs.

However, Safety First, a substance abuse reduction program affiliated with the Drug Policy Alliance, argues that zero tolerance policies fail to protect teens from the harms of substance abuse and may, in fact, have the opposite effect. Researcher Michael D. Resnick discovered during the late 1990s that healthy relationships between teens and the adults in their families and schools led to low rates of substance abuse. As a result of zero tolerance policies, teens are frequently separated from these supportive relationships, say critics, thereby increasing the likelihood that their use of drugs or alcohol will escalate. For example, a student kicked off the basketball team for smoking marijuana may no longer have access to the coach who had been encouraging him to go to college. In addition, a British government report from 2003 noted that zero tolerance policies can hurt teens by encouraging them to hide, rather than seek treatment for, true substance abuse problems.

Critics also assert that zero tolerance programs that require substance abuse treatment for every violation escalate drug use by putting non-addicts in close contact with teens who are serious addicts. Data from the Substance Abuse and Mental Health Services Administration shows that between 1990 and 2000, more than 1 million teens were excluded from school or school activities for drug policy violations. Admissions to adolescent treatment centers increased by two-thirds during the same decade due to zero tolerance policies. According to Joel Brown, a researcher with the Center for Educational Research and Development in Berkeley, California, more than 90 percent of teens in mandated treatment are not addicts but curious experimenters or occasional users who were caught using marijuana. Critics argue that these teens are vulnerable to encouragement or coercion to expand their drug use by hard-core users in treatment programs.

To be sure, zero tolerance policies remain highly controversial. The authors in the following chapter examine these policies and other factors that may promote teen drug abuse. That a policy to reduce teen substance abuse might actually increase it has prompted some experts to examine these policies more critically. Whether or not schools will end their zero tolerance policies remains to be seen, however.

I *"Drug addiction is a disease."*

# Addiction Is a Brain Disease

### National Institute on Drug Abuse

*In the following viewpoint taken from a Web site for teens, the National Institute on Drug Abuse (NIDA) describes how drugs affect the chemical reactions that take place in the brain. According to NIDA, drugs work on the reward center of the brain, altering dopamine levels, which makes the user feel good. Once drug use stops, NIDA contends, the user feels depressed because his or her brain no longer produces enough dopamine. Thus, as drugs alter the brain, users must continue to use in order to feel good. The National Institute on Drug Abuse is part of the U.S. government's National Institutes of Health, within the Department of Health and Human Services. Its mission is to conduct and promote scientific research as a foundation for understanding drug abuse, addiction, and treatment.*

As you read, consider the following questions:

1. Why is the effect of drugs on the limbic system of the brain called the "reward" system, according to NIDA?
2. According to the author, when does the brain begin to change in response to the use of a drug?

"The Brain and Addiction," *NIDA for Teens*, National Institute on Drug Abuse, 2003.

3. According to NIDA, how must addiction be treated?

The brain is the command center of your body. It weighs about three pounds, and has different centers or systems that process different kinds of information.

The brainstem is the most primitive structure at the base of your brain. The brainstem controls your heart rate, breathing, and sleeping; it does the things you never think about.

Various parts or lobes of the brain process information from your sense organs: the occipital lobe receives information from your eyes, for example. And the cerebral cortex, on top of the whole brain, is the "thinking" part of you. That's where you store and process language, math, and strategies: It's the thinking center. Buried deep within the cerebral cortex is the limbic system, which is responsible for survival: It remembers and creates an appetite for the things that keep you alive, such as good food and the company of other human beings.

The cerebellum is responsible for things you learn once and never have to think about, such as balance when walking or how to throw a ball.

## How Does Your Brain Work?

The brain's job is to process information. Brain cells called neurons receive and send messages to and from other neurons. There are billions of neurons in the human brain, each with as many as a thousand threadlike branches that reach out to other neurons.

In a neuron, a message is an electrical impulse. The electrical message travels along the sending branch, or axon, of the neuron. When the message reaches the end of the axon, it causes the release of a chemical called a neurotransmitter. The chemical travels across a tiny gap, or synapse, to other neurons.

Specialized molecules called receptors on the receiving neuron pick up the chemical. The branches on the receiving

## Brain Changes Are Part of the Disease of Addiction

The fact is, drug addiction is a *brain disease*, [director of the National Institute on Drug Abuse Alan] Leshner says. "While every type of drug of abuse has its own individual trigger for affecting or transforming the brain, many of the results of the transformation are strikingly similar regardless of the addictive drug used. The brain changes range from fundamental and long-lasting changes in the biochemical makeup of the brain, to mood changes, to changes in memory processes and motor skills."

Hazelden Voice, *Winter 2001.*

end of a neuron are called dendrites. Receptors there have special shapes so they can only collect one kind of neurotransmitter.

In the dendrite, the neurotransmitter starts an electrical impulse. Its work done, the chemical is released back into the synapse. The neurotransmitter then is broken down or is reabsorbed into the sending neuron.

Neurons in your brain release many different neurotransmitters as you go about your day thinking, feeling, reacting, breathing, and digesting. When you learn new information or a new skill, your brain builds more axons and dendrites first, as a tree grows roots and branches. With more branches, neurons can communicate and send their messages more efficiently.

## What Do Drugs Do to the Brain?

Some drugs work in the brain because they have a similar size and shape as natural neurotransmitters. In the brain in the right amount or dose, these drugs lock into receptors and start an unnatural chain reaction of electrical charges, causing neurons to release large amounts of their own neurotransmitter.

Some drugs lock onto the neuron and act like a pump, so the neuron releases more neurotransmitter. Other drugs block reabsorption or reuptake and cause unnatural floods of neurotransmitter.

All drugs of abuse, such as nicotine, cocaine, and marijuana, primarily affect the brain's limbic system. Scientists call this the "reward" system. Normally, the limbic system responds to pleasurable experiences by releasing the neurotransmitter dopamine, which creates feelings of pleasure.

## What Happens If Someone Keeps Using Drugs?

Think about how you feel when something good happens—maybe your team wins a game, you're praised for something you've done well, or you drink a cold lemonade on a hot day—that's your limbic system at work. Because natural pleasures in our lives are necessary for survival, the limbic system creates an appetite that drives you to seek those things.

The first time someone uses a drug of abuse, he or she experiences unnaturally intense feelings of pleasure. The limbic system is flooded with dopamine. Of course, drugs have other effects, too; a first-time smoker may also cough and feel nauseous from toxic chemicals in a tobacco or marijuana cigarette.

But the brain starts changing right away as a result of the unnatural flood of neurotransmitters. Because they sense more than enough dopamine, for example, neurons begin to reduce the number of dopamine receptors. Neurons may also make less dopamine. The result is less dopamine in the brain: This is called down regulation. Because some drugs are toxic, some neurons may also die.

## Becoming an Addict

No one knows how many times a person can use a drug without changing his or her brain and becoming addicted.

A person's genetic makeup probably plays a role. But after enough doses, an addicted teen's limbic system craves the drug as it craves food, water, or friends. Drug craving is made worse because of down regulation.

Without a dose of the drug, dopamine levels in the drug abuser's brain are low. The abuser feels flat, lifeless, depressed. Without drugs, an abuser's life seems joyless.

Now the abuser needs drugs just to bring dopamine levels up to normal levels. Larger amounts of the drug are needed to create a dopamine flood or high, an effect known as tolerance.

By abusing drugs, the addicted teen has changed the way his or her brain works. Drug abuse and addiction lead to long-term changes in the brain. These changes cause addicted drug users to lose the ability to control their drug use. Drug addiction is a disease.

## If Drug Addiction Is a Disease, Is There a Cure?

There is no cure for drug addiction, but it is a treatable disease; drug addicts can recover. Drug addiction therapy is a program of behavior change or modification that slowly retrains the brain. Like people with diabetes or heart disease, people in treatment for drug addiction learn behavioral changes and often take medications as part of their treatment regimen.

*"[T]here is not one iota of evidence'
that addiction is a brain disease."*

# Addiction Is Not a
# Brain Disease

## Citizens Commission on Human Rights

*The Citizens Commission on Human Rights (CCHR) was
established in 1969 by the Church of Scientology to investigate
and expose what the organization considers to be psychiatric
violations of human rights. In the following viewpoint the CCHR
disputes the assertion that drug addiction is a brain disease. According to the CCHR, the psychiatric diagnosis of addiction as a
disease is merely an attempt by the American Psychiatric Association and the pharmaceutical industry to "cash in" on the
billion-dollar drug treatment industry. By calling addiction a
disease, these entities try to convince Americans that the only effective approach to drug abuse is medical intervention in the
form of drug treatment.*

As you read, consider the following questions:

1. What kinds of evidence does the CCHR offer to justify
   its dismissal of the diagnostic practices of the American

"Rehab Fraud: Psychiatry's Drug Scam," www.cchr.org, 2004. Reproduced by permission.

Psychiatric Association?

2. What psychiatric treatments are listed in the viewpoint as failed cures for drug addiction?

3. As quoted by the authors, how does psychiatrist Sally Satel characterize the relative roles of behavior and disease in the definition of addiction?

Methadone treatment is a deception and failure. Redefining drug addiction as a treatable "disease" is part of the deception. According to renowned Professor of Psychiatry Emeritus Thomas Szasz, "[T]here is not one iota of evidence" that addiction is a brain disease. Szasz says that by defining the use or abuse of illegal drugs as a "disease," this placed the treatment for it within the province of the psychiatrist. Psychiatrists then describe the course of this "untreated disease"—"steady deterioration leading straight to the insane asylum"—and prescribe its "treatment": "psychiatric coercion with or without the use of additional, 'therapeutic' drugs (heroin for morphine; methadone for heroin . . .)."

The American Psychiatric Association's *Diagnostic and Statistical Manual of Mental Disorders IV (DSM-IV)* and Europe's *International Classification of Diseases (ICD)*, mental disorders section provide all-inclusive listings, lumping together everything from alcohol, amphetamines, cannabis, cocaine, hallucinogens, inhalants, nicotine, sedatives and hypnotics to caffeine. The *DSM-IV* lists "Substance Dependence," "Substance Abuse" and "Substance Intoxication" to cover the various types of "mental disorders" related to these substances. There's even "Substance-Induced Anxiety Disorder."

This generalized classification gives rise to some outrageously false psychiatric claims: "24% of American men have a lifetime diagnosis of Alcohol Abuse or Alcohol Dependence," and "24.1% of the population, or 48.2 million Americans, have some kind of mental disorder." The media quote these bold pronouncements as fact. However, in their book *Making*

## Addiction Is Not a Disease

Addiction is not a brain disease, nor is it caused by chemical imbalance or genetics. Addiction is best viewed as an understandable, unconscious, compulsive use of psychoactive materials in response to abnormal prior life experiences, most of which are concealed by shame, secrecy, and social taboo.

*Vincent J. Felitti,* The Origins of Addiction, *2003.*

*Us Crazy,* Professors Herb Kutchins and Stuart A. Kirk say, "Such statistics come from studies that are based on *DSM*'s inadequate definition of mental disorder. . . . *DSM* is used to directly affect national health policy and priorities by inflating the proportion of the population that is defined as 'mentally disordered.'" The numbers are also used to "shape mental health policy and the allocation of federal and state revenues."

Michael First, one of the developers of the *DSM-IV*, is quoted as saying that the *DSM* "provides a nice, neat way of feeling you have control over mental disorders," but he confessed this is "an illusion."

In 2001, Canadian psychologist Tana Dineen, author of *Manufacturing Victims*, said, "Addiction treatment is a cash cow of the psychology industry, which has argued, in most cases successfully, that treatment of the 'disease' ought to be covered by health insurance."

As for Leshner's claim that addiction is a "brain disease," in his 2001 book, *Pharmocracy*, Professor Szasz says, "Psychiatrists maintain that our understanding of mental illnesses as brain diseases is based on recent discoveries in neuroscience, made possible by imaging techniques for diagnosis and pharmacological agents for treatment. This is not true."

Pediatric neurologist Fred Baughman, Jr., says that "'biological psychiatry' has yet to validate a single psychiatric condition/diagnosis as an abnormality/disease, or as anything 'neurological,' 'biological,' 'chemically imbalanced' or 'genetic.'"

In 1998, the late Loren Mosher, M.D., a member of the American Psychiatric Association for 30 years, wrote that there is no evidence confirming "brain disease attribution." Elliot S. Valenstein, Ph.D., author of *Blaming the Brain* is unequivocal: "The theories are held onto not only because there is nothing else to take their place, but also because they are useful in promoting drug treatment."

The obvious conclusion, then, is that due to their drug rehabilitation failures, psychiatry redefined drug addiction as a "treatable brain disease," making it conveniently "incurable" and requiring massive additional funds for "research" and to maintain treatment for the addiction.

## More Celebrated Poor Results

Since the 1950s, psychiatry has monopolized the field of drug rehabilitation research and treatments. Its long list of failed cures has included lobotomies, insulin shock, psychoanalysis and LSD.

"Ultra Rapid Opiate Detoxification," a more recent example, uses narcotics to keep an addict unconscious for about five hours, during which withdrawal supposedly takes place. One recipient of this treatment told of awaking, her mouth and throat blood-filled, with broken capillaries in her face, and tremendous cramping, nausea and convulsions.

In Russia, between 1997 and 1999, 100 psychosurgery operations were conducted on teenage addicts in St. Petersburg. "They drilled my head without any anesthetic," Alexander Lusikian said. "They kept drilling and cauterizing [burning] exposed areas of my brain . . . blood was everywhere. . . . During the three or four days after the operation . . . the pain in my head was so terrible—as if it had been beaten with a baseball bat. And when the pain passed a little, I still felt the desire to take drugs." Within two months, Alexander had reverted to drugs.

In 2001, Russian addicts were also strapped to beds and beaten while being fed only bread and water during withdrawl. At the Leningrad Regional Center of Addictions, alcoholics and heroin addicts are administered ketamine, an anesthetic with strong hallucinogenic properties, in conjunction with "talk therapy."

As bizarre as it may sound, Russia, Switzerland and the United States are also conducting LSD trials for substance abuse.

In 1992, Australian psychiatrists called for heroin, cocaine and marijuana to be sold legally in liquor stores. Instead, eight years later, Australia established legal "heroin injections rooms" known as "shooting galleries."

The last thing any psychiatric treatment has achieved is rehabilitation.

As reported in a 2001 survey of American companies about the effectiveness of "substance abuse" programs for their employees, "the overwhelming majority saw few results from these programs. In the survey, 87% reported little or no change in absenteeism since the programs began and 90% saw little or no changes in productivity ratings."

## "Harm Reduction" Harms

But its failures notwithstanding, psychiatry plows ahead with another justification—"harm reduction" —the idea that "drug abuse is a human right and that the only compassionate response is to make it safer to be an addict." This has led to such infamous developments as Australia's "shooting galleries," Switzerland and Germany's "needle parks" and Holland's needle exchange programs.

In the mid-1990s, Baltimore proclaimed that harm reduction would be more effective than law enforcement. The results were tragic. Baltimore's drug-overdose death rate rose to become five times that of New York City's. Its homicide rate was six times greater.

According to psychiatrist Sally Satel, "Harm reduction holds that drug abuse is inevitable, so society should try to minimize the damage done to addicts by drugs (disease, overdose) and to society by addicts (crime, health care costs). . . . But since harm reduction makes no demands on addicts, it consigns them to their addiction, aiming only to allow them to destroy themselves in relative 'safety'—and at taxpayers' expense."

While the National Institute of Drug Abuse might claim that addiction is a "chronic, relapsing brain disease," Dr. Satel calls this "pessimistic." Candidly she states, "When the treatment system doesn't do a good job, you just fall back on that [excuse]." She insists that addiction is fundamentally a problem with behavior, over which addicts can have voluntary control.

Dr. Tana Dineen, Ph.D. states: "It seems, whatever the results," addiction treatment in psychology's and psychiatry's hands, "is identifiably a business that ignores its failures. In fact its failures lead to more business. Its technology, based on continued recovery, presumes relapses. Recidivism is used as an argument for further reading . . . ."

Harm reduction and psychiatric or psychological drug rehab programs overlook the real victims—the mother who loses a child through a drug overdose, the family that can't go out at night because of neighborhood drug gangs and the many others who live in fear of drug violence.

> "Children who take Ritalin are 'three times more likely to develop a taste for cocaine,' and . . . 'are more likely to smoke as adults.'"

# Ritalin Leads to Drug Abuse

### Robert W. Lee

*Robert W. Lee is an essayist and researcher for the* New American, *a biweekly magazine published by the John Birch Society. In the following viewpoint he asserts that the use of Ritalin in childhood leads to addiction and the use of other drugs in adulthood. By being put on Ritalin for behavioral problems, youths begin to believe that drugs can solve any physical or mental problem, an attitude that can lead to drug abuse later in life. Lee also contends that the diagnostic criteria for Attention Deficit and Hyperactivity Disorder (ADHD), for which Ritalin is the primary drug of treatment, are imprecise and inconsistent. He claims that sales of Ritalin increased nearly 500 percent during the 1990s despite no universal agreement as to whether ADHD actually exists.*

As you read, consider the following questions:

Robert W. Lee, "Prescription for Addiction," *The New American*, vol. 17, February 12, 2001. Copyright © 2001 American Opinion Publishing Incorporated. Reproduced by permission.

1. According to Lee, how does Ritalin affect the central nervous system?

2. How is Ritalin being used as a recreational drug, in the author's opinion?

3. Why is Ritalin dangerous, according to Lee?

The use of drugs such as Ritalin as a panacea for the problems of today's youth brings with it many dangerous side effects, not the least of which is conditioning for future drug abuse.

In a nationally televised speech on September 14, 1986, President Ronald Reagan called for a crusade against drug abuse. "In this crusade, let us not forget who we are," said Mr. Reagan. "Drug abuse is a repudiation of everything America is. The destructiveness and human wreckage mock our heritage." Joining her husband that day was First Lady Nancy Reagan, who pleaded with America's children to "just say no" to drugs. From that moment on the war against drugs became a high-profile project of the United States government. It still is.

A major component of the war on drugs is the effort to keep illegal narcotics out of the hands of children. Across the nation the DARE (Drug Abuse Resistance Education) program has for years asked children to pledge to "keep their body free from drugs." Meanwhile, signs proclaiming a "Drug Free School Zone" can be found near schools all over the nation. Our culture, however, sends a mixed message to our nation's children on the topic of drugs. While school-age children are taught to fear illegal drugs like cocaine, heroin, and marijuana, they are increasingly taught to rely on legal drugs to ameliorate their physical and psychological problems.

## Learning to Medicate

During their early years, many if not most children are formally introduced to the drug culture by their pediatricians, where they first learn from a major authority figure outside the family that the solution to feeling "bad" is to take a drug that will make them feel "good."

The late Dr. Robert Mendelsohn, M.D., a distinguished pediatrician who served as chairman of the Illinois State Medical Licensure Board and taught at Northwestern University and the University of Illinois college of medicine, lamented this fact in his best-selling book *How to Raise a Healthy Child ... In Spite of Your Doctor*. Therein Dr. Mendelsohn complained that the "pediatrician's wanton prescribing of powerful drugs indoctrinates children from birth with the philosophy of a 'pill for every ill.'"

The pill of choice for the ills of today's children is Ritalin, a drug that is most emblematic of the mixed message our culture is sending to children about the use of drugs. Ritalin is the trademark name for methylphenidate hydrochloride, a white, crystalline powder that stimulates the central nervous system. Its effects are similar to amphetamines, and it is listed by the federal Drug Enforcement [Administration] [DEA] as a Schedule II controlled substance. That classification (which also includes opium, codeine, morphine, and cocaine) covers narcotic, stimulant, and depressant drugs that require (except in emergencies) written, non-refillable prescriptions.

Ritalin is legally prescribed to control what the psychiatric establishment currently labels Attention Deficit Hyperactivity Disorder (ADHD), the symptoms of which include short attention span, impulsive behavior, and difficulty focusing and sitting still. There is no precise or consistent diagnostic test for ADHD, and some authorities question whether it even exists. The decision whether or not to drug a child is largely based on the child's behavior as observed by parents, teachers, and physicians. According to the American Academy of Pediatrics, nearly four million schoolchildren have been diagnosed with ADHD, and at least two million are taking Ritalin (roughly double the number since 1990). It remains unclear why

# THE 3 R's

READING  'RITING  RITALIN

Rex Babin. Reproduced by permission.

roughly three times as many boys as girls manifest symptoms of the supposed disorder. Between 1990 and 1999, Ritalin sales in the U.S. increased by nearly 500 percent. Ninety percent of the world's supply of the drug is consumed here . . . .

## Ritalin and Addiction

As Dr. Mendelsohn has pointed out, the very use of such drugs as Ritalin to solve the perceived problems of childhood—in Ritalin's case, problems which used to be solved with good old-fashioned discipline—sends a message to children that it is alright to use drugs to solve problems. "Doctors are *directly* responsible for hooking millions of people on prescription drugs," Mendelsohn says. "They are also *indirectly* responsible for the plight of millions more who turn to drugs because they were taught at an early age that drugs can cure anything—including psychological and emotional conditions—that ails them." But Ritalin itself may be addictive and its use in children may physiologically prime the pump, so to speak, for later drug abuse.

Ritalin, you will recall, is classified in the same restricted category as cocaine. The *New Scientist* for April 18, 1998 reported that "some researchers are warning that regularly giving children a cocaine-like substance might prime them for drug abuse later in life." A 1995 study, published in the *Archives of General Psychiatry* found that the distribution of Ritalin in the human brain was "almost identical to that of cocaine," the only significant difference being that it took more than four times as long for Ritalin to leave the body. Other data cited by *New Scientist* indicated that children who take Ritalin are "three times more likely to develop a taste for cocaine," and that "children who take Ritalin are more likely to smoke as adults."

Medical authorities remain divided about Ritalin's addictive attributes. According to the *Brown University Child & Adolescent Behavior Letter* for March 1996, members of the Vienna, Austria–based International Narcotics Control Board believe that the "use of Ritalin . . . carries the risk of adolescent addiction. . . ." Information posted on the Yahoo! Internet health site states that "Methylphenidate may be habit-forming. Withdrawal symptoms may occur after you stop taking methylphenidate." The site warns: "Do not stop taking this medicine suddenly without asking your doctor. You may need to take smaller and smaller doses before completely stopping the medicine." But a March 29, 2000 National Institute on Drug Abuse release stated that "research funded by the National Institute of Mental Health has shown that people with ADHD do not get addicted to their stimulant medications at treatment dosages." So what are parents to believe? The cocaine-like attributes of Ritalin, including withdrawal symptoms, are well-documented, indicating that the drug may indeed be addictive.

That Ritalin can encourage further drug abuse is evidenced by the fact that it is popular as a recreational drug of choice on the streets. For years, parents have been advised to seek blood tests for their children suspected of abusing it. Some youngsters on legally prescribed Ritalin reportedly hide, rather than take, their pills and sell them to others. In 1998, the teaching certificate of an elementary school teacher in Texas was challenged after he admitted that he had melted down and "shot up" prescription Ritalin stolen from his students.

## Ritalin Abuse Among Teens

In a March 29, 2000 release, the National Institute on Drug Abuse catalogued some of the ways in which the drug is being abused:

- "In Chicago, some stimulant users mix Ritalin (or West Coast) with heroin, or with both cocaine and heroin for a more potent effect."
- "In Detroit and Minneapolis/St. Paul, middle and high school students crush and inhale the drug or take the pill orally."
- "In Phoenix, some adults have been admitted to treatment programs for abusing the drug from their children's prescriptions."
- "In Boston, according to reports by youth treatment providers, adolescents continue to abuse the drug, which is most easily available through diverted prescriptions. Drug abuse treatment staffs in Boston also report an increase in abuse among adults."

On May 5, 2000, the Associated Press reported that Ritalin's "street names include 'Vitamin R' and 'R-Ball,' and federal drug enforcers list it among the top controlled prescription drugs reported stolen in the United States." Moreover, the Drug Enforcement Administration "lists Ritalin . . . as one of the agency's 'drugs of concern.'" Indeed, the DEA "counted nearly 2,000 cases of methylphenidate theft from January 1990 to May 1995—ranking the drug among the top 10 controlled pharmaceuticals most frequently reported stolen." And, in a

1997 Indiana University survey of 44,232 students, "Nearly 7 percent of high school students surveyed reported using Ritalin recreationally at least once in the previous year, and 2.5 percent reported using it monthly or more often."

Data gleaned from emergency room admissions also confirms the plague of Ritalin abuse. A study by the federal Substance Abuse and Mental Health Services Administration found, as summarized by the Associated Press, that "in 1995 and 1996, patients ages 10 to 14 were just as likely to mention methylphenidate as cocaine in a drug-related emergency room episode." And nearly "75 percent said they had been using the drug for psychic effects or recreation." Such data prove Dr. Mendelsohn's point and underscore the hypocrisy of fighting a "war on drugs" while conditioning children to accept drug use for behavior modification by prescribing psychotropic drugs like Ritalin . . . .

Despite all the problems with Ritalin, on August 3, 2000 the *New York Times* reported that the Food and Drug Administration has approved a 12-hour tablet form of the drug to treat ADHD. Called "Concerta," it can be taken in the morning to keep youngsters drugged all day, thereby avoiding the inconvenience of periodic trips to school nurses for medication (Ritalin requires two or three doses daily). "In tests of the drug," the *Times* noted, "the most common side effects were headaches. Less common were respiratory tract infection and stomachache." Perhaps the most serious side effect, that of conditioning for future illegal drug abuse, was not mentioned.

*"Children who take Ritalin . . . cut their risk of future substance abuse by 50 percent compared with untreated ADHD children."*

# Ritalin Does Not Lead to Drug Abuse

### Michael Fumento

*Michael Fumento is a journalist, science columnist, attorney, and senior fellow at the Hudson Institute in Washington, D.C. In the following viewpoint he acknowledges that many prominent commentators, politicians, and policy makers who share his conservative political views dismiss the validity of Ritalin as a safe and effective treatment for Attention Deficit and Hyperactivity Disorder. Based on personal experience and extensive research, however, Fumento defends the usefulness of Ritalin in treating the disorder, which he believes is real. Fumento also refutes conservatives' claims that taking Ritalin leads to drug abuse later in life. On the contrary, he asserts, the drug helps youths deal with life's problems more effectively, thereby reducing the likelihood that these individuals will eventually turn to drugs to feel good.*

As you read, consider the following questions:

1. According to Fumento, why do many conservative commentators doubt the validity of ADHD?

2. How does Fumento counter arguments that Ritalin and related drugs are just pharmaceutical shortcuts for parents and teachers who don't want to be bothered teaching children self-control?

3. How does the author address charges that Ritalin is just another name for "kiddie cocaine?"

It's both right-wing and vast, but it's not a conspiracy. Actually, it's more of an anti-conspiracy. The subject is Attention Deficit Disorder (ADD) and Attention Deficit Hyperactivity Disorder (ADHD), closely related ailments (henceforth referred to in this article simply as ADHD). Rush Limbaugh declares it "may all be a hoax." Francis Fukuyama devotes much of one chapter in his latest book, *Our Posthuman Future*, to attacking Ritalin, the top-selling drug used to treat ADHD. Columnist Thomas Sowell writes, "The motto used to be: 'Boys will be boys.' Today, the motto seems to be: 'Boys will be medicated.'" And Phyllis Schlafly explains, "The old excuse of 'my dog ate my homework' has been replaced by 'I got an ADHD diagnosis.'" A March 2002 article in *The Weekly Standard* summed up the conservative line on ADHD with this rhetorical question: "Are we really prepared to redefine childhood as an ailment, and medicate it until it goes away?"

Many conservative writers, myself included, have criticized the growing tendency to pathologize every undesirable behavior—especially where children are concerned. But, when it comes to ADHD, this skepticism is misplaced. As even a cursory examination of the existing literature or, for that matter, simply talking to the parents and teachers of children with ADHD reveals, the condition is real, and it is treatable. And, if you don't believe me, you can ask conservatives who've come face to face with it themselves.

## Myth: ADHD Isn't a Real Disorder

The most common argument against ADHD on the right is also the simplest: It doesn't exist. Conservative columnist Jonah Goldberg thus reduces ADHD to "ants in the pants." Sowell equates it with "being bored and restless." Fukuyama protests, "No one has been able to identify a cause of ADD/ADHD. It is a pathology recognized only by its symptoms." And a conservative columnist approvingly quotes Thomas Armstrong, Ritalin opponent and author, when he declares, "ADD is a disorder that cannot be authoritatively identified in the same way as polio, heart disease or other legitimate illnesses."

The Armstrong and Fukuyama observations are as correct as they are worthless. "Half of all medical disorders are diagnosed without benefit of a lab procedure," notes Dr. Russell Barkley, professor of psychology at the College of Health Professionals at the Medical University of South Carolina. "Where are the lab tests for headaches and multiple sclerosis and Alzheimer's?" he asks. "Such a standard would virtually eliminate all mental disorders."

Often the best diagnostic test for an ailment is how it responds to treatment. And, by that standard, it doesn't get much more real than ADHD. The beneficial effects of administering stimulants to treat the disorder were first reported in 1937. And today medication for the disorder is reported to be 75 to 90 percent successful. "In our trials it was close to ninety percent," says Dr. Judith Rapoport, director of the National Institute of Mental Health's Child Psychiatry Branch, who has published about 100 papers on ADHD. "This means there was a significant difference in the children's ability to function in the classroom or at home."

Additionally, epidemiological evidence indicates that ADHD has a powerful genetic component. University of Colorado researchers have found that a child whose identical twin has the disorder is between eleven and 18 times more

## What's Good About Ritalin?

Whenever you consider the proper approach to treating ADHD, drugs are always on the agenda. The reason is that they work. They work very well. The current research shows that between 75–95% of children improve on stimulant medication. No other treatment, whether conventional or alternative is that effective. Because of these results, methylphenidate, known commercially as Ritalin, has become the treatment of choice for many patients with ADHD. Ritalin is but one of a number of short-term stimulants used to treat ADHD . . . .

These drugs:

- Enhance attention
- Control impulsive behavior
- Improve physical coordination
- Reduce hyperactivity
- Reduce aggression
- Reduce disruptive behavior
- Decrease activity
- Improve peer acceptance
- Increase parental praise

These drugs are a godsend. They give ADHD children and adults a chance to function somewhat normally for at least a short time during their day.

*Anthony Kane, http://addadhdadvances.com.*

likely to also have it than is a non-twin sibling. For these reasons, the American Psychiatric Association (APA), American

Medical Association, American Academy of Pediatrics, American Academy of Child Adolescent Psychiatry, the surgeon general's office, and other major medical bodies all acknowledge ADHD as both real and treatable.

## Myth: ADHD Is Part of a Feminist Conspiracy

Many conservatives observe that boys receive ADHD diagnoses in much higher numbers than girls and find in this evidence of a feminist conspiracy. (This, despite the fact that genetic diseases are often heavily weighted more toward one gender or the other.) Sowell refers to "a growing tendency to treat boyhood as a pathological condition that requires a new three R's—repression, re-education and Ritalin." Fukuyama claims Prozac is being used to give women "more of the alpha-male feeling," while Ritalin is making boys act more like girls. "Together, the two sexes are gently nudged toward that androgynous median personality . . . that is the current politically correct outcome in American society." George Will, while acknowledging that Ritalin can be helpful, nonetheless writes of the "androgyny agenda" of "drugging children because they are behaving like children, especially boy children." Anti-Ritalin conservatives frequently invoke Christina Hoff Sommers's best-selling 2000 book, *The War Against Boys*. You'd never know that the drug isn't mentioned in her book—or why.

"Originally I was going to have a chapter on it," Sommers tells me. "It seemed to fit the thesis." What stopped her was both her survey of the medical literature and her own empirical findings. Of one child she personally came to know she says, "He was utterly miserable, as was everybody around him. The drugs saved his life."

## Myth: ADHD Is Part of the Public School System's Efforts to Warehouse Kids

"No doubt life is easier for teachers when everyone sits around quietly," writes Sowell. Use of ADHD drugs is "in the school's interest to deal with behavioral and discipline problems [because] it's so easy to use Ritalin to make kids compliant: to get them to sit down, shut up, and do what they're told," declares Schlafly. The word "zombies" to describe children under the effects of Ritalin is tossed around more than in a B-grade voodoo movie.

Kerri Houston, national field director for the American Conservative Union and the mother of two ADHD children on medication, agrees with much of the criticism of public schools. "But don't blame ADHD on crummy curricula and lazy teachers," she says. "If you've worked with these children, you know they have a serious neurological problem." In any case, Ritalin, when taken as prescribed, hardly stupefies children. To the extent the medicine works, it simply turns ADHD children into normal children. "ADHD is like having thirty televisions on at one time, and the medicine turns off twenty-nine so you can concentrate on the one," Houston describes. "This zombie stuff drives me nuts! My kids are both as lively and as fun as can be."

## Myth: Parents Are Merely Doping Up Problem Children

Limbaugh calls ADHD "the perfect way to explain the inattention, incompetence, and inability of adults to control their kids." Addressing parents directly, he lectures, "It helped you mask your own failings by doping up your children to calm them down."

Such charges blast the parents of ADHD kids into high orbit. That includes my Hudson Institute colleague (and fellow conservative) Mona Charen, the mother of an eleven-year-old with the disorder. "I have two non-ADHD children, so it's not a matter of parenting technique," says Charen. "People without such children have no idea what it's like. I can tell the difference between boyish high spirits and pathological hyperactivity. . . . These kids bounce off the walls.

Their lives are chaos; their rooms are chaos. And nothing replaces the drugs."

Barkley and Rapoport say research backs her up. Randomized, controlled studies in both the United States and Sweden have tried combining medication with behavioral interventions and then dropped either one or the other. For those trying to go on without medicine, "the behavioral interventions maintained nothing," Barkley says. Rapoport concurs: "Unfortunately, behavior modification doesn't seem to help with ADHD." (Both doctors are quick to add that ADHD is often accompanied by other disorders that are treatable through behavior modification in tandem with medicine.)

## Myth: Ritalin Is "Kiddie Cocaine"

One of the paradoxes of conservative attacks on Ritalin is that the drug is alternately accused of turning children into brain-dead zombies and of making them Mach-speed cocaine junkies. Indeed, Ritalin is widely disparaged as "kiddie cocaine." Writers who have sought to lump the two drugs together include Schlafly, talk-show host and columnist Armstrong Williams, and others whom I hesitate to name because of my long-standing personal relationships with them.

Mary Eberstadt wrote the "authoritative" Ritalin-cocaine piece for the April 1999 issue of *Policy Review*, then owned by the Heritage Foundation. The article, "Why Ritalin Rules," employs the word "cocaine" no fewer than twelve times. Eberstadt quotes from a 1995 Drug Enforcement [Administration] (DEA) background paper declaring methylphenidate, the active ingredient in Ritalin, "a central nervous system (CNS) stimulant [that] shares many of the pharmacological effects of amphetamine, methamphetamine, and cocaine." Further, it "produces behavioral, psychological, subjective, and reinforcing effects similar to those of d-amphetamine, including increases in rating of euphoria, drug liking and activity, and decreases in sedation." Add to this the fact that the Controlled

Substances Act lists it as a Schedule II drug, imposing on it the same tight prescription controls as morphine, and Ritalin starts to sound spooky indeed.

What Eberstadt fails to tell readers is that the DEA description concerns methylphenidate *abuse*. It's tautological to say abuse is harmful. According to the DEA, the drugs in question are comparable when "administered the same way at comparable doses." But ADHD stimulants, when taken as prescribed, are neither administered in the same way as cocaine nor at comparable doses. "What really counts," says Barkley, "is the speed with which the drugs enter and clear the brain. With cocaine, because it's snorted, this happens tremendously quickly, giving users the characteristic addictive high." (Ever seen anyone pop a cocaine tablet?) Further, he says, "There's no evidence anywhere in literature of [Ritalin's] addictiveness when taken as prescribed." As to the Schedule II listing, again this is because of the potential for it to fall into the hands of abusers, not because of its effects on persons for whom it is prescribed. Ritalin and the other anti-ADHD drugs, says Barkley, "are the safest drugs in all of psychiatry." (And they may be getting even safer: A new medicine just released called Strattera represents the first true non-stimulant ADHD treatment.)

Indeed, a study just released in the journal *Pediatrics* found that children who take Ritalin or other stimulants to control ADHD cut their risk of future substance abuse by 50 percent compared with untreated ADHD children. The lead author speculated that "by treating ADHD you're reducing the demoralization that accompanies this disorder, and you're improving the academic functioning and well-being of adolescents and young adults during the critical times when substance abuse starts."

> "The natural extension of [the medical marijuana] myth is that, if marijuana is medicine, it must also be safe for recreational use."

# Medical Marijuana Laws Encourage Teens to Use Cannibis

*Karen P. Tandy*

*In the following viewpoint Karen P. Tandy argues that the public debate over whether marijuana should be legalized for medical use has led to an increase of cannibis use among teens. Because of the debate, Tandy asserts, teens have come to believe that smoking marijuana is healthy. In fact, she contends, most health experts refute the idea that marijuana is a medicine and stress the many dangers associated with its use. Tandy is employed by the U.S. Drug Enforcement Administration and chairs the International Association of Chiefs of Police Narcotics and Dangerous Drugs Committee.*

As you read, consider the following questions:

1. According to Tandy, what kinds of health problems are caused by marijuana?

2. Why should marijuana use not be legalized, in the author's view?

3. According to Tandy, what kinds of government-supported research has been conducted to determine the medical usefulness of marijuana?

When 14-year-old Irma Perez of Belmont, California, took a single ecstasy pill one evening last April [2004], she had no idea she would become one of the 26,000 people who die every year from drugs. Irma took ecstasy with two of her 14-year-old friends in her home. Soon after taking the tiny blue pill, Irma complained of feeling awful and said she felt like she was "going to die." Instead of seeking medical care, her friends called the 17-year-old dealer who supplied the pills and asked for advice. The friends tried to get Irma to smoke marijuana, but when she couldn't because she was vomiting and lapsing into a coma, they stuffed marijuana leaves into her mouth because, according to news sources, "they knew that the drug is sometimes used to treat cancer patients."

Irma Perez died from taking ecstasy, but compounding that tragedy was the deadly decision to use marijuana to "treat" her instead of making what could have been a lifesaving call to 911. Irma was a victim of our society's stunning misinformation about marijuana—a society that has come to believe that marijuana use is not only an individual's free choice but also is good medicine, a cure-all for a variety of ills. A recent poll showed that nearly three-fourths of Americans over the age of 45 support legalizing marijuana for medical use.

## Teens Believe Marijuana Is Safe

It's a belief that has filtered down to many of our teens, if what I'm hearing during my visits with middle school and high school students across the country is true. I'm amazed at how well versed in drug legalization these teens are. It is as if legalization advocates stood outside their schools handing out their leaflets of lies. Here is what students have told me about marijuana: "It's natural because it grows in the ground, so it must be good for you." "It must be medicine, because it makes me feel better." "Since everybody says it's medicine, it is."

Legalization advocates themselves have alluded to the fact that so-called medical marijuana is a way of achieving wholesale drug legalization. A few years ago, the *New York Times* interviewed Ethan Nadelmann, director of the Lindesmith Center, a drug policy research center. Responding to criticism that the so-called medical marijuana issue is a stalking horse for drug legalization, Mr. Nadelmann did not disagree. "Will it help lead toward marijuana legalization?" he asked. "I hope so. . . ."

The natural extension of this myth is that, if marijuana is medicine, it must also be safe for recreational use. This pervasive mindset has even reached our courts. In January 2005, for example, Governor Frank Murkowski of Alaska had to ask the legislature "to overrule a court ruling that adult Alaskans have the right to possess marijuana for personal use in their homes." There was no pretense of medical use in this ruling; it gave Alaskans the legal right to smoke marijuana for any reason, lending credence to the belief that marijuana is not only safe to treat serious illness but somehow safe for general use and for all society.

What is the antidote? Spreading the truth. . . . America is not suffering from anything that the truth can't cure. To help you set the record straight, this article seeks to rebut the rhetoric and recap the reality.

## Medical Treatment?

*Myth: Marijuana is medicine.*

*Reality: Smoked marijuana is not medicine.* The scientific and medical communities have determined that smoked marijuana is a health danger, not a cure. There is no medical evidence that smoking marijuana helps patients. In fact, the Food and Drug Administration (FDA) has approved no medications that are smoked, primarily because smoking is a poor way to deliver medicine. Morphine, for example has proven to be a medically valuable drug, but the FDA does not endorse smoking opium or heroin.

Congress enacted laws against marijuana in 1970 based in part on its conclusion that marijuana has no scientifically proven medical value, which the U.S. Supreme Court affirmed more than 30 years later in *United States v. Oakland Cannabis Buyer's Cooperative, et al.,* (2001). Marijuana remains in schedule 1 of the Controlled Substances Act because it has a high potential for abuse, a lack of accepted safety for use under medical supervision, and no currently accepted medical value.

The American Medical Association has rejected pleas to endorse marijuana as medicine, and instead urged that marijuana remain a prohibited schedule 1 drug at least until the results of controlled studies are in. The National Multiple Sclerosis Society stated that studies done to date "have not provided convincing evidence that marijuana benefits people with MS" and does not recommend it as a treatment. Further, the MS Society states that for people with MS "long-term use of marijuana may be associated with significant serious side effects."

The British Medical Association has taken a similar position, voicing "extreme concern" that downgrading the criminal status of marijuana would "mislead" the public into thinking that the drug is safe to use when, "in fact, it has been linked to greater risk of heart disease, lung cancer, bronchitis, and emphysema."

## Researchers Explore Alternatives to Smoking Marijuana

In 1999 the Institute of Medicine (IOM) undertook a landmark study reviewing the alleged medical properties of marijuana. Advocates of so-called medical marijuana frequently tout this study, but the study's findings decisively undercut their arguments. In truth, the IOM explicitly found that marijuana is not medicine and expressed concern about patients' smoking it because smoking is a harmful drug-delivery system. The IOM further found that there was no scientific evidence that smoked marijuana had medical value, even for the chronically ill, and concluded that "there is little future in smoked marijuana as a medically approved medication." In fact, the researchers who conducted the study could find no medical value to marijuana for virtually any ailment they examined, including the treatment of wasting syndrome in AIDS patients, movement disorders such as Parkinson's disease and epilepsy, or glaucoma.

The IOM found that THC (the primary psychoactive ingredient in marijuana) in smoked marijuana provides only temporary relief from intraocular pressure (IOP) associated with glaucoma and would have to be smoked eight to 10 times a day to achieve consistent results. And there exists another treatment for IOP, as the availability of medically approved once- or twice-a-day eye drops makes IOP control a reality for many patients and provides round-the-clock IOP reduction. For two other conditions, nausea and pain, the report recommended against marijuana use, while suggesting further research in limited circumstances for THC but not smoked marijuana.

Before any drug can be marketed in the United States, it must undergo rigorous scientific scrutiny and clinical evaluation overseen by the FDA. For example, the FDA has approved Marinol (dronabinol)—a safe capsule form of synthetic THC that meets the standard of accepted medicine and has the same properties as cultivated marijuana without the high—for the treatment of nausea and vomiting associated with cancer chemotherapy and for the treatment of wasting syndrome in AIDS patients.

The federal government has approved and continues to approve research into the possible use of marijuana as medicine and any new delivery systems of marijuana's active ingredients. To quote U.S Supreme Court Justice Stephen Breyer's remarks during the November 2004 *Raich* v. *Ashcroft* oral argument, "Medicine by regulation is better than medicine by referendum." Proving that the regulatory process does work, the DEA [Drug Enforcement Administration] has registered every researcher who meets FDA standards to use marijuana in scientific studies. Since 2000, for example, the California-based Center for Medicinal Cannabis Research (CMCR) has gained approval for 14 trials using smoked marijuana in human beings and three trials in laboratory and animal models. This CMCR research is the first effort to study the medical efficacy of marijuana. But researchers have not endorsed smoking marijuana and instead are attempting to isolate marijuana's active ingredients to develop alternative delivery systems to smoking. Not one of these researchers has found scientific proof that smoked marijuana is medicine.

## Legalizing Marijuana Leads to Increased Use Among Teens

*Myth: Legalization of marijuana in other countries has been a success.*

*Reality: Liberalization of drug laws in other countries has often resulted in higher use of dangerous drugs.* Over the past decade, drug policy in some foreign countries, particularly those in Europe, has gone through some dramatic changes toward greater liberalization with failed results. Consider the experience of the Netherlands, where the government reconsidered its legalization measures in light of that country's

## Early Start

Kids are using marijuana at an earlier age. In the late 1960s fewer than half of those using marijuana for the first time were under 18. By 2001, about two-thirds (67 percent) of marijuana users were younger than 18.

*Office of National Drug Control Policy,* Marijuana Prevention Initiative, *2004. www.ndcp.gov.*

experience. After marijuana use became legal, consumption nearly tripled among 18- to 20-year-olds. As awareness of the harm of marijuana grew, the number of cannabis coffeehouses in the Netherlands decreased 36 percent in six years. Almost all Dutch towns have a cannabis policy, and 73 percent of them have a no-tolerance policy toward the coffeehouses.

In 1987 Swiss officials permitted drug use and sales in a Zurich park, which was soon dubbed Needle Park, and Switzerland became a magnet for drug users the world over. Within five years, the number of regular drug users at the park had reportedly swelled from a few hundred to 20,000. The area around the park became crime-ridden to the point that the park had to be shut down and the experiment terminated.

Marijuana use by Canadian teenagers is at a 25-year peak in the wake of an aggressive decriminalization movement. At the very time a decriminalization bill was before the House of Commons, the Canadian government released a report showing that marijuana smoking among teens is "at levels that we haven't seen since the late '70s when rates reached their peak." After a large decline In the 1980s, marijuana use among teens increased during the 1990s, as young people apparently became "confused about the state of federal pot laws."

*Myth: Marijuana is harmless.*

*Reality: Marijuana is dangerous to the user.* Use of marijuana has adverse health, safety, social, academic, economic, and behavioral consequences; and children are the most vulnerable to its damaging effects. Marijuana is the most widely used illicit drug in America and is readily available to kids. Compounding the problem is that the marijuana of today is not the marijuana of the baby boomers 30 years ago. Average THC levels rose from less than 1 percent in the mid-1970s to more than 8 percent in 2004. And the potency of B.C. Bud, a popular type of marijuana cultivated in British Columbia, Canada, is roughly twice the national average-ranging from 15 percent THC content to 20 percent or even higher.

*Marijuana use can lead to dependence and abuse.* Marijuana was the second most common illicit drug responsible for drug treatment admissions in 2002—outdistancing crack cocaine, the next most prevalent cause. Shocking to many is that more teens are in treatment each year for marijuana dependence than for alcohol and all other illegal drugs combined. This is a trend that has been increasing for more than a decade: in 2002, 64 percent of adolescent treatment admissions reported marijuana as their primary substance of abuse, compared to 23 percent in 1992.

*Marijuana is a gateway drug.* In drug law enforcement, rarely do we meet heroin or cocaine addicts who did not start their drug use with marijuana. Scientific studies bear out our anecdotal findings. For example, the *Journal of the American Medical Association* reported, based on a study of 300 sets of twins, that marijuana-using twins were four times more likely than their siblings to use cocaine and crack cocaine, and five times more likely to use hallucinogens such as LSD. Furthermore, the younger a person is when he or she first uses marijuana, the more likely that person is to use cocaine and heroin and become drug-dependent as an adult. One study found that 62 percent of the adults who first tried marijuana before they were 15 were likely to go on to use cocaine. In contrast, only 1 percent or less of adults who never tried marijuana used heroin or cocaine.

*Smoking marijuana can cause significant health problems.* Marijuana contains more than 400 chemicals, of which 60 are cannabinoids. Smoking a marijuana cigarette deposits about three to five times more tar into the lungs than one filtered tobacco cigarette. Consequently, regular marijuana smokers suffer from many of the same health problems as tobacco smokers, such as chronic coughing and wheezing, chest colds, and chronic bronchitis. In fact, studies show that smoking three to four joints per day causes at least as much harm to the respiratory system as smoking a full pack of cigarettes every day. Marijuana smoke also contains 50 to 70 percent more carcinogenic hydrocarbons than tobacco smoke and produces high levels of an enzyme that converts certain hydrocarbons into malignant cells.

In addition, smoking marijuana can lead to increased anxiety, panic attacks, depression, social withdrawal, and other mental health problems, particularly for teens. Research shows that kids aged 12 to 17 who smoke marijuana weekly are three times more likely than nonusers to have suicidal thoughts. Marijuana use also can cause cognitive impairment, to include such short-term effects as distorted perception, memory loss, and trouble with thinking and problem solving. Students with an average grade of D or below were found to be more than four times as likely to have used marijuana in the past year as youths who reported an average grade of A. For young people, whose brains are still developing, these effects are particularly problematic and jeopardize their ability to achieve their full potential.

*Myth: Smoking marijuana harms only the smokers.*

*Reality: Marijuana use harms nonusers.* We need to put to rest the thought that there is such a thing as a lone drug user, a person whose habits affect only himself or herself. Drug use, including marijuana use, is not a victimless crime. Some in your communities may resist involvement because they think someone else's drug use is not hurting them. But this kind of not-my-problem thinking is tragically misguided. Ask those same people about secondhand smoke from cigarettes, and they'll quickly acknowledge the harm that befalls nonsmokers. Secondhand smoke is a well-known problem, one that Americans are becoming more unwilling to bear. We need to apply the same common-sense thinking to the even more pernicious secondhand effects of drug use.

> "The decrease in teen marijuana use in medical marijuana states has slightly exceeded the national decline."

# Medical Marijuana Laws Do Not Encourage Teens to Use Cannibis

*Karen O'Keefe and Mitch Earleywine*

*In the following viewpoint Karen O'Keefe and Mitch Earleywine assert that medical marijuana laws do not increase the recreational use of marijuana among teens. In fact, they maintain, such laws can reduce adolescent marijuana use. Their argument is based on an analysis of publicly available research data from ten states that have enacted medical marijuana use laws since 1996. Their research predates the June 2005 U.S. Supreme Court ruling that holds that state medical marijuana laws may be superseded by federal law. O'Keefe is a legislative analyst for the Marijuana Policy Project and Earleywine is associate professor of psychology at the State University of New York at Albany.*

As you read, consider the following questions:

1. According to O'Keefe and Earleywine, what is the "wrong message" argument that is used by those who oppose laws allowing the medical use of marijuana?

2. Which federal drug use surveys were used to compile the data analyzed by the authors?

3. According to data presented by the authors, how do the trends for teen marijuana use in states with medical marijuana laws compare with national usage trends?

Nine years after the passage of the nation's first state medical marijuana law, California's Prop. 215, a considerable body of data shows that no state with a medical marijuana law has experienced an increase in youth marijuana use since their law's enactment. All have reported overall decreases of more than the national average decrease—exceeding 50% in some age groups—strongly suggesting that enactment of state medical marijuana laws does not increase teen marijuana use.

## Experience in the States

1. In California—which has the longest-term, most detailed data available—the number of ninth graders reporting marijuana use in the last 30 days declined by 47% from 1996 (when the state's medical marijuana law passed) to 2004. An analysis commissioned by the California Department of Alcohol and Drug Programs found "no evidence supporting that the passage of Proposition 215 increased marijuana use during this period."

2. In Washington state, sixth graders' current and lifetime marijuana use has dropped by at least 50% since the 1998 enactment of the state's medical marijuana law. All other surveyed grade levels have seen both lifetime and current marijuana use drop by between 25% and 50%.

3. In Hawaii, youth marijuana use has decreased among all surveyed grade levels—by as much as 38%—since the 2000 passage of the state's medical marijuana law.

4. Data from Maine suggest a modest decline since the 1999 passage of its law. Data from Nevada (whose law was passed in 2000) and Alaska (whose law was passed in 1998) show overall decreases in marijuana use, with a modest increase in a few individual grade levels. Data from Oregon (whose law passed in 1998) suggest modest declines in marijuana use among the two grades surveyed in 2004, a slight decrease in lifetime marijuana use among high schoolers, and a tiny increase in current marijuana use among high schoolers. Colorado (whose law passed in 2000) is the only state without an in-depth statewide survey, but the limited data available suggest modest declines in Colorado teens' marijuana usage as well.

5. Vermont and Montana, whose medical marijuana laws were enacted in 2004, have not yet produced statistically valid data covering the period since their laws were passed.

6. Nationwide, teenage marijuana use has decreased in the nine years since California enacted the country's first effective medical marijuana law. Overall, the trends in states with medical marijuana laws are slightly more favorable than the trends nationwide. California, Washington, and Colorado have all seen much greater drops in marijuana usage than have occurred nationwide. Overall, Alaska's and Hawaii's trends are also more favorable than nationwide trends, though some individual measures are less favorable. Trends from Maine, Oregon, and Nevada are slightly less favorable than nationwide trends, although use is still down . . . .

Since 1996, 10 states—Alaska, California, Colorado, Hawaii, Maine, Montana, Nevada, Oregon, Vermont, and Washington—have passed laws allowing the use of marijuana for medical purposes. Eight of these were enacted via voter-approved ballot measures, while Hawaii's and Vermont's laws were passed by their legislatures. (The District of Columbia passed a similar ballot initiative in 1998, but due to congressional action, the law hasn't been implemented.) In addition, medical marijuana legislation was considered during the 2005 legislative sessions of at least 16 state legislatures.

## The "Wrong Message" Argument

One argument consistently raised in opposition to such measures is that they "send the wrong message to young people," encouraging teen drug experimentation. For example, in an October 1996 letter to anti-drug advocates, U.S. Drug Enforcement Administration [DEA] Administrator Thomas A. Constantine wrote, "How can we expect our children to reject drugs when some authorities are telling them that illegal drugs should no longer remain illegal, but should be used instead to help the sick? . . . We cannot afford to send ambivalent messages about drugs."

Such arguments continue to be raised by opponents of medical marijuana laws. In June 2005, Rhode Island Gov. Donald Carcieri (R) explained his veto of a medical marijuana bill in part by arguing that the measure would "place our children at increased risk of abusing marijuana." That same month, U.S. Representatives Mark Souder (R-IN) and Frank Wolf (R-VA) raised the "wrong message" concern during a floor debate on medical marijuana in the U.S. House of Representatives.

In 1996, the issue of whether these laws would impact teen marijuana use was an open question: Both sides made assertions, but neither had concrete data for support. Now, nine years after the passage of the first medical marijuana initiative, California's Prop. 215, a considerable body of data exists. No state with a medical marijuana law has experienced an overall increase in youth marijuana use since the law's enactment. All have reported overall decreases—in some cases exceeding 50%

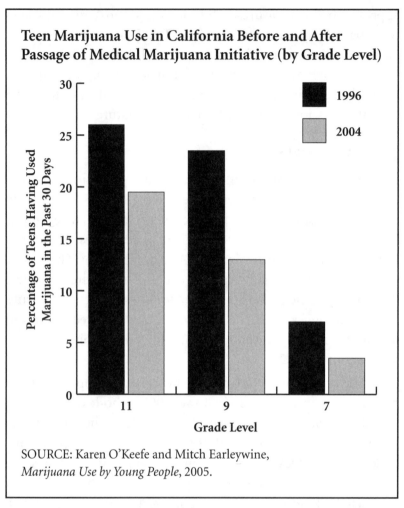

**Teen Marijuana Use in California Before and After Passage of Medical Marijuana Initiative (by Grade Level)**

SOURCE: Karen O'Keefe and Mitch Earleywine, *Marijuana Use by Young People*, 2005.

in specific age groups—strongly suggesting that the enactment of state medical marijuana laws does not increase teen marijuana use.

## Many Studies Track Marijuana Use by Teens

All of the data in this report is from state and federal government surveys of drug use by young people. The most well-known of these are the annual Monitoring the Future study, conducted by the University of Michigan under contract with the U.S. National Institute on Drug Abuse, and the National Survey on Drug Use and Health (NSDUH)—formerly called the National Household Survey on Drug Abuse (NHSDA)— conducted by the Research Triangle Institute and sponsored by the U.S. Substance Abuse and Mental Health Services Administration. However, state-specific data were not available for all 50 states from NHSDA/NSDUH until 1999, so before-and-after data are not available for many states with medical marijuana laws. Even in the cases where such data are available, the NSDUH has determined that the state-level "estimates for 2002 and later years [are] not comparable with prior years" and "the relative rankings of States may have been affected" due to methodological changes. Furthermore, the NSDUH's state samples are very small and NSDUH reports the 12- to 17-year age range as a block, rather than breaking down specific ages or grade levels.

Many states—including California, Hawaii, Maine, Oregon, and Washington—conduct detailed state-level surveys with methodology similar to NSDUH, but they use far larger samples within each state. We have included all relevant data from such surveys where available.

Also of interest is the Youth Risk Behavior Surveillance (YRBS), conducted by many (but not all) states in conjunction with the U.S. Centers for Disease Control and Prevention. The YRBS has produced data for several individual states, including Alaska, Maine, Nevada, and Oregon.

Because some surveys are conducted only every other year, and because of the time needed to collect and process data, the two states with the newest medical marijuana laws— Montana and Vermont—have not yet released results covering the period since their laws were enacted. Nevertheless, enough data are available now from the eight other medical marijuana states to draw conclusions.

Data were located through Internet searches and federal and state government agencies. In each case, we have reviewed all publicly available data from national and statewide teen drug use surveys, including the most recent figures available as of this writing, August 2005. The only results omitted from the analysis are from surveys in which the only available data are "unweighted." This occurs, for example, when school-based surveys are unable to enroll a broadly representative sample of a state's school population, meaning that the results cannot be considered statistically valid for the statewide youth population.

Most of these surveys ask whether participants have used drugs in the last 30 days (considered "current use") and ever in their life. Washington changed the wording of its question regarding lifetime drug use in the 2000 survey, but it restored the old language in 2002. Other methodological changes were also made in 2002, including the time of year when surveys were administered. Oregon made substantial changes in the methodology of its 2001 survey, which makes it more difficult to draw firm conclusions across time.

As with all polls and surveys, the surveys analyzed for this report have a statistical margin of error. (Hawaii is the exception because its data is from a census sampling that was given to all public school students whose parents returned consent forms.) The margin of error ranges from 0.3% to 9.5% (the margin of error data was not available for Washington state in 1998 and 2000 or for California's surveys).

Statements from those raising the "wrong message" concern have often been vague as to whether they believe the harm comes from actual implementation of medical marijuana laws or from the public discussion stimulated by the campaigns. Because many of their statements (including that of the DEA administrator cited above) focus on public discussion, and because the campaigns for the state laws produced intense debate and media coverage, we have focused on the date of enactment as the key time-point in before-and-after comparisons.

## Marijuana Use by Teens Has Declined, Even in States with Medical Marijuana Laws

Since California voters enacted Prop. 215, the debate over it and similar proposals has been covered widely on national television and radio, as well as in local and national newspapers and magazines, including *USA Today*'s front-page story on Prop. 215's passage; the *New York Times*' 1999 front-page story on the Institute of Medicine's report on the medical use of marijuana, and many others. If medical marijuana laws "send the wrong message" to children, this widespread attention would be expected to produce a nationwide increase in marijuana use, with the largest increase in those states enacting medical marijuana laws. But just the opposite has occurred.

Since 1996, Monitoring the Future surveys show 43%, 33%, and 9% decreases in eighth, tenth, and twelfth graders' current marijuana use, respectively. Regarding lifetime use, it shows a 29% drop in eighth graders' use, a 12% decline in tenth graders', and a 2% increase among twelfth graders. The biennial national YRBS shows similar trends, with an 11% decrease in high schoolers' current marijuana use since 1995 and a 5% decrease in their lifetime use. It found decreases in every measure in every high school grade level since 1995, except twelfth graders' lifetime marijuana use, which shows a slight increase. . . . As a whole, the medical marijuana states' teen use trends compare favorably to nationwide trends.

The Monitoring the Future survey randomly samples approximately 120 high schools nationally for twelfth grade data, surveying about 15,000 students annually. For its survey of eighth graders each year, approximately 17,000 students from 140 randomly selected schools are surveyed annually. For the tenth graders, approximately 130 high schools are sampled, and about 15,000 students are surveyed annually. The national YRBS uses a three-stage, cluster sample design to obtain a nationally representative sample of students in grades nine through [twelve] in the United States. Approximately 10,200 surveys were completed in 2003, 9,900 in 1999, 11,220 in 1997, and 6,540 in 1995.

[The data show that] states enacting medical marijuana laws have been slightly more successful than the nation as a whole at reducing adolescent marijuana use . . . .

## Do Medical Marijuana Laws Lead to a Decline in Recreational Use of Marijuana?

Since the mid-1990s, the U.S. has witnessed a well-publicized and sometimes emotional national debate over the medical use of marijuana. Contrary to the fears expressed by opponents of medical marijuana laws, there is no evidence that the enactment of 10 state medical marijuana laws has produced an increase in adolescent marijuana use in those states or nationwide. Instead, data from those states suggest a modest decline overall, with very large declines in some age groups in some states. Overall, the decrease in teen marijuana use in medical marijuana states has slightly exceeded the national decline.

In all eight states with available data covering two or more years since enactment of their medical marijuana laws, teen marijuana use declined overall, sometimes dramatically, after passage of a medical marijuana law. Only Hawaii had any data suggesting an overall increase since its law's passage, and making year-to-year comparisons before and after the relevant 2002 survey is considered invalid by the commissioning organization, the NSDUH. Further, far more comprehensive data show decreases among all surveyed ages of Hawaiian youth.

While it is not possible with existing data to determine conclusively that state medical marijuana laws caused the documented declines in adolescent marijuana use, the overwhelming downward trend strongly suggests that the effect of state medical marijuana laws on teen marijuana use has been either neutral or positive, discouraging youthful experimentation with the drug. California researchers, who appear to be the only ones to specifically study the issue in the context of a survey of adolescent drug use, found no evidence of a "wrong message" effect. The reasons for this lack of impact have not been adequately studied. Perhaps medical marijuana laws send a very different message than opponents of such laws have suggested: Marijuana is a treatment for serious illness, not a toy, and requires cautious and careful handling. Legislators considering medical marijuana proposals should evaluate the bills on their own merits, without concern for unproven claims that such laws increase teen marijuana use. Opponents of medical marijuana laws should cease making such unsubstantiated claims.

"*Parents and schools may be sending binge-drinking/social marijuana smokers off to treatment and getting back crackheads in their stead.*"

# Drug Treatment Leads to Substance Abuse

*Maia Szalavitz*

*In the following viewpoint Maia Szalavitz asserts that due to zero-tolerance policies in schools and communities, teens who use drugs only occasionally are forced into treatment programs that are designed for addicts. When teens are told by program leaders to admit that they are helpless against the power of drugs—a standard treatment approach—they lose faith in the program's efficacy. No teen believes he or she is powerless, Szalavitz claims. Moreover, she maintains, teens sent to drug treatment programs come under the influence of serious abusers also receiving treatment. These peers often encourage teens to continue using and may also help them obtain drugs upon release. Szalavitz is a senior fellow at the Statistical Assessment Service at George Mason University.*

Maia Szalavitz, "Trick or Treatment: Teen Drug Programs Turn Curious Teens into Crackheads," *Slate*, January 3, 2003. Distributed by United Feature Syndicate, Inc.

As you read, consider the following questions:

1. What are Szalavitz's primary objections to the use of twelve-step-based treatment techniques with teens who are unaddicted?

2. According to the author, what is the psychological effect of typical drug abuse treatment strategies on nonaddicted teens whose substance abuse is best considered experimental or occasional?

3. What treatment options does Szalavitz recommend for teens who must participate in a school- or court-ordered treatment program for nonaddicted substance use?

America loves its quick fixes. Think your child might be on drugs? Test him. Think your child's school is full of addicts? Test them all. Institute a policy of zero tolerance: One strike and it's off to a drug treatment program. Get those rotten apples out and clean them up before they can poison the whole batch. Last year's Supreme Court decision in *Board of Education v. Earls* [June 27, 2002] allowed for a massive expansion of drug testing in school. And increases in drug testing increase the numbers of offenders. As a result, schools and juvenile courts are increasingly turning to both "zero tolerance" and juvenile "treatment, not punishment" as a remedy.

The number of teenagers in drug treatment as a result of court coercion and school diversion increased by nearly 50 percent between 1993 and 1998 according to the U.S. Department of Health and Human Services' Substance Abuse and Mental Health Services Administration [SAMHSA], and the number of teen admissions to treatment programs in general rose from 95,000 in 1993 to 135,000 in 1999. But what if drug "treatment" doesn't work for teens? What if, rather than decreasing drug use, teen treatment actually encourages it by labeling experimenting kids as lifelong addicts? What if it creates the worst sorts of peer groups by mixing kids with mild problems with serious drug users who are ready and willing to teach them to be junkies? What if suggestible kids respond poorly to the philosophies that have made Alcoholics Anonymous and Narcotics Anonymous successful for many adults? Then we'd be using "treatment" to turn ordinary adolescents into problem drug abusers.

## From Social User to Addict?

That's precisely what we're doing. A 1998 study of nearly 150 teenagers treated in dozens of centers across the country found that there was 202 percent more crack abuse *following* treatment and a 13 percent increase in alcohol abuse. In other words, recent research suggests that parents and schools may be sending binge-drinking/social marijuana smokers off to treatment and getting back crackheads in their stead.

Michael's case illustrates some of the dangers inherent in shipping youngsters off to treatment programs. An 18-year-old marijuana smoker and cocaine user I interviewed regarding drug treatment, Michael was recently sent by his parents for drug treatment at the respected Caron Foundation. But his $11,000 one-month treatment program degenerated into a fruitless debate when his counselor wanted him to admit that he was "powerless" over drugs [a strategy similar to that of the Alcoholics Anonymous program]. Michael, who didn't use daily, wouldn't accept that. What teenager would admit to being "powerless" over anything? Michael used again within four hours of leaving treatment.

Michael's reaction may be the rule for teenagers, not the exception. For an adult who has lost his wife, his job, his health, and his home, admitting to a loss of control might help him recognize that quitting drugs is the only way to solve his problems. But a teenager may not be "in denial" when he says he can control his intake. Most teenagers can. Conversely, forcing a teen to assert that they have no control may do more harm than good, if they have only been experimenting

# Treating the Wrong Teens?

Over the past 10 years, more than one million adolescents have been removed from school for drug-policy violations, according to Joel Brown of the Center for Educational Research and Development, who is currently studying the effect schools have in forcing youths into treatment. In a great number of those cases, Brown says, students have only one way to get readmitted to school: enroll in a treatment facility. No one knows the full extent of this trend, because there are no centralized statistics kept on drug-related school expulsions. The trend does, however, seem to help explain why adolescent treatment admissions have shot up by about two-thirds since 1990, according to a recent study by the federal Substance Abuse and Mental Health Services Administration.

Brown estimates that "less than 10 percent" of the kids who enter treatment at the insistence of their schools actually have a problem . . . .

School drug policies vary by state and district. Schools usually have discretion to suspend or expel students who are caught with drugs. Some simply require a student caught with drugs to go in for an assessment. But . . . it does not take much to be diagnosed as an "abuser."

Consider these unassuming questions from the New Bridge Foundation's self assessment for teens: "Do you sometimes hang out with kids who drink/use? Have you had anything to drink in the last week? Have you ever felt guilty or bummed out after drinking/using?"

Such vague questions, many researchers say, help to explain how kids without real drug problems end up thrown in as hard-core addicts.

*Jake Ginsky, MotherJones.com, 2000. www.motherjones.com.*

with drugs but are convinced, via treatment, that they are serious addicts. If a teenager has been persuaded that she's powerless and has a 90 percent chance of relapse, she's far less likely to exercise self-control when confronted with a drink or drugs. In fact, a 1996 study published by Bill Miller, professor of psychology at the University of New Mexico, found that those adults who most accepted the idea of personal powerlessness had the most severe and dangerous relapses. Since teenage identities are fluid anyway, encouraging them to view themselves as powerless addicts may cement an anti-social identity that a teen was just trying on for size.

## Wrong Diagnosis, Wrong Cure

The core problem with teen treatment programs is that most teen drug or alcohol users are just not out-of-control addicts. More than one teen in six who's forced into treatment does not even fit the criteria for a "substance abuse disorder" (the less serious diagnosis for an abuser), and most also don't have substance dependence (the psychiatric term for addiction) at all, according to SAMHSA. More troubling, SAMHSA statistics also show that about three-quarters of the U.S. teens now being sent to treatment programs are diverted there by courts or schools, rather than being referred by professionals. In other words, many have problems no more serious than those of their friends who've escaped detection.

In addition to labeling kids as addicts, drug programs may also surround them with the worst possible influences. Studies show that teens are more subject to peer pressure than adults—and more influenced by the people around them. Teen treatment programs remove teens from a healthy peer group and surround them with other problem kids, virtually guaranteeing that their role models will be negative. Group therapy during such treatment invariably involves discussions of their drug experiences—which only makes the hard-drug users seem "cooler" because their stories are so much more exciting. Worse, aside from providing a way for relatively inexperienced kids to learn about different ways of getting high and obtaining drugs, these programs frequently offer kids new connections. One 17-year-old girl from Florida told me that she hadn't used cocaine until after treatment—her new best friend from rehab scored it for her.

## What Works?

There are treatments for teens that don't reinforce the labeling or peer problems inherent in most drug programs. Research presented at a spring conference held by the National Institute on Drug Abuse compared teens who'd been sent to traditional group sessions with peers to teens who received family therapy, with a third group who had both kinds of care combined. The kids in the peer-group sessions used 50 percent more marijuana after treatment, while the kids in the combined treatment used 11 percent more pot. The teenagers treated with their parents, however, decreased their marijuana use by 71 percent.

The greatest irony in the current well-intentioned treatment efforts is that they ignore the few things we do know to be effective in helping teens stop getting high, and chief among them is finishing their education. The better educated someone is, the less likely he is to become an addict or to have a lengthy course of addiction if he does. So removing kids from school and placing them with a more deviant peer group in an unproven therapy is madness—and not much smarter than simply expelling them and tossing them on the street. Not only is the education provided in treatment programs often inferior to that in ordinary school, but having a drug-related disciplinary record diminishes the chances of admission to a decent college.

Ultimately, it's clear that the vast majority of teenagers (even those with the very worst problems) simply "mature out" of drug use. This natural recovery process is seen in statistics from the annual federal household survey of drug use, which, for example, find that while 18.4 percent of the population ages 18–24 in 2001 qualified for a diagnosis of alcohol or other drug abuse or dependence, only 5.4 percent of those over 26 meet these criteria. Since less than 2 percent of the total population annually receives treatment (including self-help), most of these young people are clearly recovering on their own.

Why, then, do we insist on herding teenagers into inappropriate treatment programs when allowing them to finish school works better? Do parents really want their pot-smoking, experimenting binge-drinkers (who are actually typically more moderate than their own parents were at their age) tossed into "therapy" with heroin injectors and told that they are powerless to resist?

Studies show that family therapy and behavioral one-on-one counseling work better for teens than programs modeled on adult addicts. Even for kids with genuine drug addictions, these sorts of treatments may be more helpful, and it's long past time that such programs were implemented in communities rather than debated in the academy. For kids with minor drug problems or—as is more often the case—for kids who are just being kids, the philosophy must be: First, do no harm. Although we may hate the idea, leaving kids alone and letting them grow out of their habits makes far more sense than testing, punishing, and "curing" them—by making them worse.

I *"Treating alcohol and drug abuse in teens is a wise investment."*

# Drug Treatment Combats Substance Abuse

### *Judy Shepps Battle*

*Judy Shepps Battle is a writer who specializes in topics related to addiction and recovery. In this viewpoint she advocates residential treatment for teen drug abusers. She notes that recovery programs for adolescent substance abusers generally include both formal and informal peer interaction sessions and require participation in group counseling sessions. According to the author, teens in residential treatment benefit from being separated from drugs, peers, and family at the start of treatment. At the end of treatment, she notes, teens will be required to receive counseling together with their parents to ensure that upon release youths will return to a healthier home environment.*

As you read, consider the following questions:

1. What does the author identify as the "major antidote"

    for alcohol and drug use?

2. According to Battle, what is the role of predictable and consistent consequences in teen drug abuse treatment?

3. What are the important characteristics of the family counseling component of teen recovery treatment, as outlined by the author?

> It finally happened. Joan is now in a residential treatment center for her alcohol and drug problems. It was hard to send our 14-year-old daughter away but she was so out of control. Curfew meant nothing and we started noticing things missing around the house—small items like her brother's Walkman and my watch.
>
> Last weekend, she went to a friend's birthday party and passed out from acute alcohol poisoning. We were so scared that she would die. I'm not exactly sure how this treatment facility is going to help Joan, but I know her mother and I are at our wit's end.
>
> —*Mr. Robert J.*

Adolescence—even without alcohol and drug abuse—is a difficult maturational passage. It is the bridge between the dependency of childhood and adult identity. It is a time of rebellion, "trying on" adult behaviors and extensive limit-testing in all areas.

Unfortunately, when alcohol and drugs are involved, many youngsters are unable to handle the physical and emotional consequences. The limits that are broken—legal and physical—often leave a teen in dangerous situations.

Residential treatment is often the last stop for an out-of-control substance-abusing teenager. It offers a "time out" from situations that trigger self-destructive behavior, a chance to experience predictable and consistent consequences of behavior, an opportunity to participate in community, and for family bonds to be repaired. In the process, self-esteem—the major antidote to alcohol and drug use—is increased.

How does this happen? Let's follow Joan J. through several aspects of her treatment experience.

## Creating a "Time Out"

Joan's entrance into a residential facility immediately separated her from alcohol and drugs, peers using these substances and ineffective parental rules. In their place was a world that was structured, supervised, therapeutic and substance-free.

Joan was not happy with this change. She began to experience mild to moderate withdrawal symptoms and spent her first days detoxing. When this discomfort ended she was enraged at losing her freedom.

"I hate my mother and my father for putting me here. I hate myself for getting caught and not being able to handle the booze and coke. I see the other kids here kidding around with each other and hate them too."

Her parents, hearing about the daily schedule of school, community meetings, chores and therapy sessions were sure Joan would either run away or refuse to participate. But, despite her anger, Joan did not fight the new rules.

"She seems almost relieved that something bigger than her is in charge," said Mrs. J. "Maybe she is as tired of fighting as we are."

## Predictable and Consistent Consequences

The heart of most residential treatment programs is the "level system." During orientation, Joan was made aware of four stages of increasing responsibility and privileges. To advance to the next level, she had to demonstrate responsibility, self-awareness, and make a positive contribution to the general community.

She began at level one—orientation—and had no privileges. It was easy to move to level two. All she had to do was accept a job, be on time for individual and family counseling sessions, and attend community meetings, and she could leave her unit and make phone calls.

Level three required a note from her job supervisor that she was doing well, making a positive contribution to all

## Does Relapse Mean Treatment Failed?

Of all the myths and misconceptions surrounding adolescent drug use and addiction, the most damaging of all may be the belief that treatment doesn't work if the adolescent relapses or experiences continuing drug-related problems. Treatment works—but it takes time. Treatment works in the same way that seeds planted in a garden take months, even years, to grow to full maturity. With patience and tender, ongoing care, the seeds will take root; with time, the roots will become firmly entrenched.

Everyone involved in the lives of children who use drugs must understand that treatment is not a single, discrete event that stops when the adolescent leaves a structured inpatient or outpatient program. Adolescents (and adults) require a continuum of care involving ongoing assessment, intervention, and treatment at various levels of intensity, depending on the individual's present needs. Such a program of continuing care "reinforces the need for chronic attention and vigilance in response to a chronic vulnerability, even in the improved patient," writes Marc Fishman, M.D. "Ongoing treatment at less intensive levels of care to consolidate gains initiated at more intensive levels of care is a critical feature of successful treatment across a continuum of care."

*Katherine Ketcham and Nicholas A. Pace,*
Teens Under the Influence, *2003.*

counseling sessions, and participating in community meetings. Rewards included weekend family passes, the right to spend money at the commissary, and a one-hour-later bedtime.

The fourth level involved taking a leadership role in the community. It meant leading an orientation session for newcomers, writing out the reasons why she came to be in residential treatment and what needed to change when she got home so that she would not need additional residential treatment. The reward was to count down the days before she could go home and [to] enjoy a fairly nonrestrictive time on her unit.

In order to advance to a higher level, a resident had to present his case to the entire community, staff and teens. If there were negative votes, he could not advance. Each negative vote had to be explained face-to-face to the applicant.

Like most teens, Joan would advance a level or two and then break a rule and return to level one. She was testing to see if the counselors meant what they said. Once she was finally convinced of the consistency of consequences, she advanced to the fourth level.

Joan was proud of her newly acquired leadership skills, and her parents and counselors noticed the dramatic increase in her self-esteem.

## Participation in Community

Recovery from substance abuse requires that the chemical high be replaced by some other source of feeling good. In addition, the psychological pain that is medicated by alcohol and other drugs must be faced therapeutically and healed.

"I'm learning about natural highs," says Joan. "This morning we did this really neat trust exercise where we each took turns climbing a platform and falling backwards into the arms of the entire group. The first time I did it I was really scared they would drop me. But they didn't. And the second time I just shut my eyes and loved it!"

Joan also spends time daily with her counselor identifying and talking about her feelings. She is beginning to talk about how afraid she is that her parents will divorce and that no boy will ever want to date her. She loves to write in her journal and draws pictures of a little girl who used to be sad but is starting to smile.

## Repairing Family Bonds

Before a youth can go home, the bonds between parent and child so severely strained during the height of teen alcohol and drug abuse need to be repaired. This is accomplished through the involvement of family members in the treatment process.

Family therapy sessions are held on a regular basis. Feelings of anger, fear, shame and love are expressed. Strategies for conflict resolution are developed. The rules of the home are stated and clear consequences for violation outlined. A reward system is developed for good behavior. Finally, a list of therapeutic resources is drawn up in case a third party is needed for mediation.

Some facilities have an evening or a day designated as Family Day. It is a time of sharing of food, watching an educational presentation and discussing how this lesson applies to the family unit. Topics may cover the nature of addiction, self-help groups, or how families resolve conflicts.

Joan's father summed it up nicely:

"I am so happy that we found help for Joan but in reality our whole family has been positively affected by her treatment. We talk to one another and are learning to listen. Both my wife and I have decided to enter individual therapy to address our own issues. If Joan can risk growing, we can, too."

Studies consistently show that treating alcohol and drug abuse in teens is a wise investment. Not only is heavy drinking and drug use diminished but adolescents receiving treatment have fewer thoughts of suicide, lower hostility and higher self-esteem. They also report better-than-average grades.

# Periodical Bibliography

The following articles have been selected to supplement the diverse views presented in this chapter.

| Doug Brunk | "Stimulants for ADHD: No Link to Later Drug Abuse," *Family Practice News*, October 1, 2005. |
| --- | --- |
| Susan M. Gordon | "Teen Drug Abuse: Underlying Psychological Disorders and Parental Attitudes Have a Big Effect on Teens' Addictive Behaviors," *Behavioral Health Management*, September/October 2003. |
| John W. Maag and Deborah M. Irvin | "Alcohol Use and Depression Among African-American and Caucasian Adolescents," *Adolescence*, Spring 2005. |
| Lenora Marcellus | "Marijuana and Medicine: Assessing the Science Base," *Family and Community Health*, October–December 2005. |
| Marsha Rosenbaum | "Keep Teenagers Safe: Zero Tolerance on Alcohol May Increase Drinking and Driving," *San Jose Mercury News*, December 29, 2004. |
| Sandy Fertman Ryan | "Prescription for Trouble: From Middle Schoolers Lookin' for a Buzz to High School Students Attempting to Lose Weight to College Kids Pulling All Nighters, Ritalin Abuse Is Rampant," *Girls' Life*, October/November 2005. |
| Jacob Sullum | "That Chemo Cachet: Medical Marijuana and Kids," *Reason*, January 2006. |
| Curren Warf and Alain Joffe | "Response to the American Academy of Pediatrics Report on Legalization of Marijuana," *Pediatrics*, November 2005. |

OPPOSING
VIEWPOINTS®
SERIES

# CHAPTER 3

# Do the Media Promote Teen Drug Abuse?

# Chapter Preface

Teens watch a lot of television and see a lot of movies, say the authors of *Reducing Underage Drinking: A Collective Responsibility*. On a weekly basis, younger teens (ages 11 to 13) spend nearly twenty-eight hours watching television and more than six hours watching movies. Those between 14 and 18 watch just over twenty hours of television and nearly five hours of movies. According to the book, among the television programs most watched by teens, more than half (53 percent) typically portray alcohol use, usually in a favorable light (the primary message is that attractive people relax and have fun drinking alcohol). Most television and movie depictions involve drinkers of legal age, but underage drinking is frequently portrayed as a means of appearing mature or fitting in with peers. Many researchers concerned about teen drug use claim that these media depictions contribute to teen substance abuse.

These experts point out that anyone who observes young children pretending to be their favorite television characters know how on-screen action can affect real-life behavior and attitudes. They also note that retailers acknowledge the media's influence, counting on the influence of popular television shows, movies, and video games to sell their action figures, board games, lunch-boxes, and other merchandise targeted at youths. Teen clothing, make up, and hair trends mirror the sexy images portrayed in music videos and prime-time serials, and high-priced shoes and athletic gear become top-sellers when famous athletes endorse them on TV. Many researchers claim that society readily acknowledges that consumer trends in popular culture can be traced to hit television shows and blockbuster movies, thus it also should recognize the media's role in promoting teen drug abuse.

Some studies support this view. Two studies published in 2004 by the Rand Corporation suggest that what teens watch on television strongly influences their behavior in social situations. The research focused on the influence of television programming on sexual attitudes and behavior. Teens whose television choices exposed them to high levels of sexual content were found to be twice as likely to engage in sexual intercourse during the next year as teens who were exposed to the lowest levels of sexual content on television. In addition, in 2004, James Sargent, heading a team of researchers at Dartmouth Medical School, found that middle-school students exposed to numerous movie scenes in which adults are drinking are three times more likely to try drinking than are their peers who have not been exposed to these images. In 2005 Sargent's research team published the first national study to examine the relationship between young teen smoking behavior and portrayals of smoking in movies. One key finding of the study was that the 10- to-14-year-olds who were exposed to the highest levels of onscreen smoking behavior were 2.6 times more likely to become smokers than the participants who had been exposed to the fewest depictions of smoking in movies.

Not everyone agrees that the media contribute to teen drug abuse, of course, but the media's role in substance abuse problems has garnered increasing attention. The authors in the following chapter examine how media portrayals of drug use may influence teen behavior. Determining whether TV programs and movies play a role in teen addiction is critical, considering the amount of time youths spend in front of the television and in the nation's movie theaters.

| "Thanks . . . to cigarette company marketing efforts, each day more than 4,000 kids try smoking for the first time."

# Cigarette Ads Strongly Influence Teen Smoking

*Meg Gallogly*

*In the following viewpoint Meg Gallogly of the Campaign for Tobacco-Free Kids asserts that there are clear links between cigarette ads and teen smoking. She offers evidence that cigarette companies have deliberately targeted teens in their marketing efforts, despite restrictions imposed by the 1998 Master Settlement Agreement that required the industry to stop marketing to teens and children. Gallogly charges that in addition to continuing to design cigarette ads and marketing campaigns so that they will appeal to young people, the tobacco industry actively resists efforts to restrict underage access to cigarettes.*

As you read, consider the following questions:

1. What evidence is presented by Gallogly to support her argument that tobacco companies have historically targeted teens in their marketing efforts?

Meg Gallogly, "Tobacco Cobacco Company Marketing to Kids," Campaign for Tobacco Free Kids, August 9, 2005. Reproduced by permission.

2. How does the tobacco industry continue to thwart the government's efforts to restrict underage access to cigarettes, according to the author?

3. According to Gallogly, what do the findings of a 2002 study by the National Cancer Institute reveal about the relationship between tobacco marketing and the smoking behavior of teens?

The major cigarette companies, alone, now spend about $15.1 billion per year (or more than $41 million every day) to promote their products; and many of their marketing efforts directly reach kids. In fact, cigarette company spending to market their deadly products increased by almost 125 percent from 1998 to 2003 (the most recent year for which complete data is available) and partial data for 2004 show that these increases are continuing. Moreover, tobacco industry documents, research on the effect of the cigarette companies' marketing efforts on kids, and the opinions of advertising experts combine to reveal the intent and the success of the industry's efforts to attract new smokers from the ranks of children.

## Tobacco Industry Statements and Actions

Numerous internal tobacco industry documents [from the 1970s, 1980s, and early 1990s], revealed in the various tobacco lawsuits, show that the tobacco companies have perceived kids as young as 13 years of age as a key market, studied the smoking habits of kids, and developed products and marketing campaigns aimed at them. As an RJR [R.J. Reynolds] Tobacco document put it, "Many manufacturers have 'studied' the 14–20 market in hopes of uncovering the 'secret' of the instant popularity some brands enjoy to the almost exclusion of others. . . . Creating a 'fad' in this market can be a great bonanza." The following are just a few of the many more internal company quotes about marketing to kids:

**Philip Morris:** "Today's teenager is tomorrow's potential regular customer, and the overwhelming majority of smokers first begin to smoke while still in their teens. . . . The smoking patterns of teenagers are particularly important to Philip Morris."

**R.J. Reynolds:** "Evidence is now available to indicate that the 14–18 year old group is an increasing segment of the smoking population. RJR-T must soon establish a successful new brand in this market if our position in the industry is to be maintained in the long term."

**Brown & Williamson:** "Kool's stake in the 16- to 25-year-old population segment is such that the value of this audience should be accurately weighted and reflected in current media programs . . . all magazines will be reviewed to see how efficiently they reach this group."

**Lorillard Tobacco:** "[T]he base of our business is the high school student."

**U.S. Tobacco:** "Cherry Skoal is for somebody who likes the taste of candy, if you know what I'm saying."

## Tobacco Communities Still Market Their Products to Kids

The cigarette companies now claim that they have finally stopped *intentionally* marketing to kids or targeting youths in their research or promotional efforts. But they continue to advertise cigarettes in ways that reach vulnerable underage populations. For example, the cigarette and spit-tobacco companies continue to advertise heavily at retail outlets near schools and playgrounds, with large ads and signs clearly visible from outside the stores. In addition:

- A study in the *New England Journal of Medicine* found that the 1998 Master Settlement Agreement has had little effect on cigarette advertising in magazines. In 2000, the tobacco companies spent $59.6 million in advertising expenditures for the most popular youth brands in youth-oriented magazines. The settlement has not reduced youth exposure to advertisements for these brands. Magazine ads for each of the three most popular youth brands (Marlboro, Newport, and Camel) reached more than 80 percent of young people in the United States an average of 17 times in 2000.

- Similarly, a Massachusetts Department of Health study found that cigarette advertising in magazines with high youth readership actually increased by 33% after the November, 1998 Master Settlement Agreement, in which the tobacco companies agreed not to market to kids. And an American Legacy Foundation study found that magazine ads for eight of the top ten cigarette brands reached 70 percent or more of kids five or more times in 1999.

- In June of 2002, a California judge fined the R.J. Reynolds cigarette company for advertising in magazines with high youth readerships in ways that violated the state tobacco settlement agreement's prohibition that forbids the cigarette companies from taking any action directly or indirectly to target youth in the advertising, promotion, or marketing of tobacco products.

- In July 2000, a study revealed that after tobacco billboards were banned by the Master Settlement Agreement the cigarette companies increased their advertising and promotions in and around retail outlets, such as convenience stores.

- According to a study conducted by the Massachusetts Department of Health, United States Smokeless Tobacco Company (USST), the country's largest smokeless tobacco manufacturer, spent $9.4 million advertising in magazines with high youth readership in 2001, compared to the average $5.4 million spent in 1997 and

1998, the two years before the settlement. Nearly half of the company's advertising (45 percent) continued to be in youth-oriented magazines after the settlement.

At the same time, major cigarette companies vigorously oppose reasonable efforts to make it more difficult for kids to obtain cigarettes—such as raising tobacco excise taxes, eliminating cigarette vending machines in locations accessible by children, requiring that tobacco products be sold from behind the counter, forbidding sales of single cigarettes or "kiddie packs" (packs of fewer than 20 cigarettes), or prohibiting sales of cigarettes via the internet or through the mail.

In fact, the cigarette companies are addicted to underage smoking. Almost 90 percent of all regular smokers begin smoking at or before age 18, and hardly anybody tries their first cigarette outside of childhood. In other words, if kids stopped smoking, the cigarette companies market of smokers would shrink away to almost nothing. But thanks, in large part, to cigarette company marketing efforts, each day more than 4,000 kids try smoking for the first time, and another 2,000 kids become regular daily smokers.

## Evidence of the Impact of Tobacco Marketing to Kids

Beyond the industry's own statements, there is compelling evidence that much of their advertising and promotion is directed at kids and successfully recruits new tobacco users. A 2002 monograph by the National Cancer Institute [NCI], which reviewed the research on tobacco advertising and promotion and its impact on youth smoking, found that tobacco advertising and promotional activities are important catalysts in the smoking initiation process. The NCI report also found, based on a review of the extant research, that "the conclusion that there is a causal relationship between tobacco marketing and smoking initiation seems unassailable."

Wright. Reproduced by permission.

A number of studies have demonstrated the relationship between tobacco marketing and youth smoking behavior:

- 82 percent of youth (12–17) smokers prefer Marlboro, Camel and Newport—three heavily advertised brands. Marlboro, the most heavily advertised brand, constitutes almost 50 percent of the youth market but only about 38 percent of smokers over age 25.

- A study in the *American Journal of Public Health* showed that adolescents who owned a tobacco promotional item and named a cigarette brand whose advertising attracted their attention were twice as likely to become established smokers than those who did neither.

- A study released in March 2005 showed that kids were more than twice as likely as adults to recall tobacco advertising. While only 26 percent of all adults recalled seeing a tobacco ad in the two weeks prior to the survey, 56 percent of kids aged 12 to 17 reported seeing tobacco ads.

- A 2002 study in the *Archives of Pediatric and Adolescent Medicine* found that receptivity to tobacco advertising had a significant impact on each step of the progression from non-smoking to established regular smoking, even when exposure to smoking in the home and by peers was controlled. The biggest impact was on influencing non-susceptible youth to becoming susceptible to smoking.

- A study in the *Journal of the National Cancer Institute* found that teens are more likely to be influenced to smoke by cigarette advertising than they are by peer pressure.

- A study in the *Journal of Marketing* found that teenagers are three times as sensitive as adults to cigarette advertising.

- A longitudinal study of teenagers in the *Journal of the American Medical Association* showed that tobacco industry promotional activities influenced previously non-susceptible non-smokers to become susceptible to or experiment with smoking.

- An *American Journal of Preventive Medicine* study found that youth who were highly receptive to advertising were 70 percent more likely to move from being experimental smokers to established smokers compared to those who had a minimal receptivity to tobacco advertising. The study also found that youth who believed that they could quit smoking anytime were almost twice as likely to become established smokers compared to those who did not think they could quit any time.

- According to the U.S. Centers for Disease Control and Prevention, the development and marketing of "starter products" with such features as pouches and cherry flavoring have switched smokeless tobacco from a product used primarily by older men to one used mostly by young men. More than 14 percent of high school boys are current smokeless tobacco users.

- In the early 1980's, 30 percent of kids 12 to 17 years old, both smokers and nonsmokers owned at least one tobacco-brand promotional item, such as T-shirts, backpacks, and CD players.

- Between 1989 and 1993, when advertising for the new Joe Camel campaign jumped from $27 million to $43 million, Camel's share among youth increased by more than 50 percent, while its adult market share did not change at all.

- A report in the *Journal of the American Medical Association* documented a rapid and unprecedented increase in the smoking initiation rate of adolescent girls subsequent to the launch in the late 1960's of women's cigarette brands like Virginia Slims.

- A December 1996 survey of advertising industry executives found that roughly 80 percent believed that advertising for cigarettes reaches children and teenagers in significant numbers and makes smoking more appealing or socially acceptable to kids. And 71 percent believed that tobacco advertising changes behavior and increases smoking among kids; and 59 percent believe that a goal of tobacco advertising is marketing cigarettes to teenagers who do not already smoke.

As a commentator in the *Advertising Age* trade journal put it, "Cigarette people maintain peer pressure is the culprit in getting kids to start smoking and that advertising has little effect. That's like saying cosmetic ads have no effect on girls too young to put on lipstick."

> *"[Cigarette] advertisements may not have the strong impact that previous research has suggested."*

# Cigarette Ads Do Not Strongly Influence Teen Smoking

*Alyse R. Lancaster and Kent M. Lancaster*

*In the following viewpoint Alyse R. Lancaster and Kent M. Lancaster assert that magazine-based cigarette advertising has a minimal effect on teen smoking. According to the authors, youths must encounter such advertising three or more times before it influences them, but adolescents rarely read that many cigarette ads. They contend that the best way to reduce teen smoking is not to ban cigarette advertising targeting teens but to present more antismoking messages on TV and on the Internet. Alyse R. Lancaster and Kent M. Lancaster are professors at the University of Miami School of Communication.*

As you read, consider the following questions:

1. What do the authors say about the effects on teens of

nonprint media messages about cigarettes?

2. According to the data presented by the Lancasters, what percentage of teens are likely to be exposed to three or more of a cigarette brand's magazine ads?

3. According to the authors, which factors are more likely than magazine advertising to influence a teenager's decision to start smoking?

Following the 1971 broadcast ban on tobacco advertising, magazines have become an important medium for tobacco advertisers in the United States. In 1999, major tobacco advertisers spent approximately $442.7 million on magazine advertising. Research suggests that because magazines are targeted specifically to particular demographic groups, it is easier for advertisers, particularly tobacco advertisers, to reach various segments of the population, including women and children.

## The Relationship Between Smoking Behavior and Advertising

Historically, as tobacco advertising campaigns became more targeted, smoking rates among targeted groups tended to increase. For example, tobacco companies began targeting women in the mid 1920s as more women began smoking during that period. This trend strengthened in the 1960s, when tobacco companies developed marketing campaigns designed specifically for women. Many researchers argue that the same logic can be applied to targeting youth. Young people who report being aware of tobacco promotions are likely to be more susceptible to using tobacco products, and are encouraged to begin smoking. In addition, images in cigarette ads rely on adventure, risk, and recreation rather than on the unhealthy side effects of smoking, and these images potentially diminish perceived risks of smoking. In a longitudinal study of the association between receptivity to tobacco advertising and promotion and the initiation of smoking, [researcher John P.] Pierce et al. (1998) concluded that there is a positive relationship between the two variables and that exposure to cigarette advertising can influence nonsmokers to begin smoking and become addicted to cigarettes.

One of the biggest questions surrounding teen smoking is whether cigarette usage among teens stems from exposure to cigarette advertising. Magazines are a popular medium for advertising tobacco products, and several studies have suggested that tobacco advertisers use magazines that reach children and young adults. Other studies further argue that there is indeed a relationship between exposure to tobacco advertising and smoking among teens. For example, [Richard W.] Pollay et al. (1996) found a positive relationship between cigarette brand selection and exposure to brand advertising among teenagers. Pierce et al. (1998) found that teens who are receptive to cigarette advertising are more likely to smoke than those who are not receptive to the advertising . . . .

## Measuring Exposure to Cigarette Advertising

Several studies have concluded that cigarette advertising in magazines reaches teenagers. [Cheryl L.] Albright et al. (1988) found that the number of magazines with youth readership that accept cigarette advertising increased from 1971 (following the broadcast ban) until 1985. [Charles] King et al. (1998) reported that cigarette brands popular among adolescents are more likely to be advertised in magazines than adult brands. Pierce et al. (1998) concluded that promotional tobacco activities, including magazine advertising, are causally related to the onset of smoking among adolescents.

A recent study by [Karen Whitehall] King and [Michael] Siegel (2001) examined trends in advertising expenditures for 15 cigarette brands and exposure of young people to cigarette advertising in 38 youth-oriented magazines between 1995 and

153

2000. Youth-oriented magazines were assumed to have more than 15% of their readership comprised of teen readers, or at least 2 million readers who were between 12 and 17 years old. They found that the proportion of young people who were potentially exposed to cigarette advertising in magazines ranged from 81.9 to 88.4% for youth-brand cigarettes and from 55.5 to 80.1% for adult brands. They further found that the proportion of young people who were potentially exposed three or more times in a given year ranged from 61.3 to 87.9%. The average frequency of potential magazine advertising ranged from 10.2 to 32.8 magazine exposures per year. Throughout their study, the authors are careful to state that their analysis refers only to potential exposure to the cigarette advertisements contained within the magazines studied; they did not attempt to estimate exposure to cigarette advertisements themselves.

In an analysis similar to that performed by King and Siegel, [Dean M.] Krugman and King (2000) also examined teens' exposure to consumer magazines that contained cigarette advertising. Their analysis examined 14 consumer magazines that contain cigarette advertising and have a youth readership of at least 15%. Assuming one insertion in each of the 14 magazines, they found that approximately 66.1% of teens would be reached by the magazines an average of 2.1 times. By gender, they found that these magazines reached approximately 78% of male readers and 52.9% of female readers between 12 and 17 years old. However, these figures refer to magazine reach, not message reach, which is also the case in the King and Siegel (2001) study. In other words, they refer to exposure to a magazine carrying cigarette advertisements, and not to the cigarette advertisements themselves . . . .

The important issue is whether teens are being exposed not to the magazines themselves, but rather, to the cigarette ads contained within them. Not all people who read a magazine will read all of the ads contained within it. Hence,

## Freedom of Speech vs. an Advertising Ban

"Fundamentally," writes Jean J. Boddewyn, a professor of marketing at Baruch College, "one cannot prove that advertising does *not* cause or influence smoking, because one cannot scientifically prove a negative." So despite the lack of evidence that advertising has a substantial impact on smoking rates, tobacco's opponents can argue that we should play it safe and ban the ads—just in case.

Since we clearly are not helpless to resist the persuasive powers of Philip Morris et al.—all of us see the ads, but only some of us smoke—it is hard to square an advertising ban with a presumption against censorship. Surely a nation that proudly allows racist fulminations, communist propaganda, flag burning, nude dancing, pornography, and sacrilegious art can safely tolerate Marlboro caps and Joe Camel T-Shirts.

*Jacob Sullum, "Cowboys, Camels, and Kids," Reason Online, 1998. www.reasononline.com.*

vehicle (magazine) reach is not the equivalent of message (advertisement) reach.

In addition to determining message reach, researchers must also consider the number of advertising exposures to estimate advertising effectiveness. Substantial academic and industry research has suggested that multiple exposures to a message are needed to communicate key message content. . . . The present study examines both magazine and cigarette advertising reach and frequency using the same set of consumer magazines that were analyzed in the Krugman and King study. . . .

# Results of the Analysis

[The current study compiled data showing] three levels of analysis based on both SMRB [Simmons Market Research Bureau, Inc.] and MRI [Mediamark Research, Inc.] magazine audience estimates, including results for the publications themselves, for full-page, four-color advertisements for all products combined . . . and for cigarette advertisements in particular. As with the Krugman and King (2000) study, the analysis assumes one use of each of the 14 magazines. For purposes of estimating advertisement coverage, the analysis is assumed to encompass one typical brand or cigarette advertiser using one full-page, four-color advertisement in each of the 14 magazines over a one-month time frame. . . .

Although 66.1% of teens are likely to be exposed to 1 or more of the 14 publication issues, only 46.1% are likely to be exposed to one or more full-page, four-color advertisement for a typical brand if the readership norm for all product categories combined is used. If the cigarette readership norm is used, it is estimated that only 41.4% of teens are likely to be exposed to one or more full-page, four-color advertisement for a typical cigarette brand within the 14 publications.

Advertising scholars and practitioners have long recognized the role of frequency in achieving advertising communication effects. . . . [A common estimate is] that three or more message exposures are required to be effective. Other frequency levels could certainly be analyzed as well, but three is used here as an example since it is one of the thresholds that is most typically used and studied. . . .

It is estimated that 59.5% of teens are likely to be exposed to 1 or more of the 14 magazines, 39.2% are likely to be exposed to 1 or more of a typical brand's advertisements, and 34.9% are likely to be exposed to 1 or more of a typical cigarette brand's advertisements. Approximately 13.0% of teens are estimated to look into or read 3 or more of the 14 magazines, whereas only 2.3% are likely to see 3 or more of a typical brand's advertisements, and only 1.5% are likely to see 3 or more of a typical cigarette brand's advertisements . . . .

## What Do the Results Mean?

Tobacco advertising often is cited as a primary reason why teens smoke. This reasoning would assume that teens not only are exposed to a particular brand's cigarette advertisements, but are exposed to them enough times for the advertisements to have a behavioral impact. The results of this study suggest that if traditional media-planning methods are applied specifically to teen reading of tobacco advertising in consumer magazines, potential message impact may be minimal, even when substantially larger annual schedules are analyzed. Although approximately 59.5–66.1% of teens are likely to be exposed to 1 or more of the 14 magazines in this study, depending on whether MRI or SMRB data are used, only approximately 13.0–20.5% of teens are likely to be exposed to 3 or more magazines. More important to note is that approximately 34.9–41.4% of teens are likely to be exposed to one or more full-page, four-color cigarette advertisement(s) for a typical brand within these magazines. Only 1.5–2.7% of teens are likely to be exposed to three or more of a typical cigarette brand's advertisements in the 14 magazines.

Perhaps the study of the media effects of cigarette advertising and of antismoking efforts on teens should not be limited to consumer magazines, as other media appear to have an influence on smoking behaviors as well. [Cornelia] Pechmann and [Chuan-Fong] Shih (1999) found that positive images of smokers in movies might drive teens to begin smoking. [Michael] Siegel and [Lois] Biener (2000) concluded that the addition of a television component to an antismoking campaign aimed at adolescents may reduce the initiation of smoking, particularly among younger teens.

## Ads in Media Other than Magazines

The 1999 National Youth Tobacco Survey questioned middle- and high-school students about exposure to media and advertising regarding tobacco. Their results were presented in four categories: (1) saw antismoking commercials on television or heard them on the radio, (2) saw actors smoking on television or in the movies, (3) saw athletes smoking on television, and (4) saw ads for tobacco products on the Internet. It is interesting to note that the survey did not appear to question respondents about exposure to magazine advertising. On average, approximately 87.3% of students saw actors smoking, and 75.3% saw antismoking commercials. These findings suggest that perhaps traditional cigarette advertisements such as those placed in consumer magazines do not contribute to youth smoking as much as other factors do and that more effective antismoking efforts may be in order.

## Are Antismoking Messages More Effective?

The 75.3% of youth that reported seeing antismoking commercials in broadcast media is higher than the magazine reach figures reported in the Krugman and King (2000) study, and in addition, they refer to actual messages, not vehicles. If it is assumed that exposure to cigarette advertising leads to an increase in smoking, then using the same logic, it can likely be assumed that exposure to equally well-designed antismoking advertisements will lead to a decrease in smoking.

This is consistent with the results of several econometric studies that look at the effects of tobacco advertising on tobacco consumption. A number of studies have concluded that over time, tobacco advertising has a limited impact on increasing the incidence of smoking and that bans on tobacco advertising are not effective in significantly reducing cigarette smoking.

In fact, several of these studies conclude that antismoking messages and health scares seem to be more effective at reducing smoking rates than bans on tobacco advertising. This suggests that if greater effort were placed on developing antismoking messages specifically targeted to youth smokers instead of banning or limiting tobacco advertising, the role of mass media in the decline of youth smoking might be strengthened.

This phenomenon already appears to have taken effect. For example, a recent antismoking campaign in Florida, the "Truth" campaign, has been coupled with a reduction in smoking among Florida teens. In fact, the *Journal of the American Medical Association* reported that in the first two years of the campaign, smoking among students in Florida declined by 40% among middle-school students and by 18% among high-school students . . . .

## How Much Influence Comes from Media Messages?

It is important to note that a teen's decision not to smoke or to discontinue smoking usually is driven by variables other than media messages. Although antismoking campaigns may contribute to a reduction in the number of teens who smoke, other factors have been shown to be highly influential as well. Peer pressure, family influence, gender, and ethnicity all may have an impact on the onset of smoking among youth. While each of these factors plays a role in a teen's decisions to smoke or abstain from smoking, perhaps the most important one is the price of cigarettes. Because most teens have low disposable incomes, the increasing cost of cigarettes and rising taxes on them often serve as a deterrent to the onset of smoking, more so than other influences. Given that price is such an important factor in a teen's decision to smoke or abstain from smoking, perhaps antismoking efforts aimed at teens should begin to focus on the high monetary cost of smoking relative to other activities of interest to teens.

Public service campaigns have often been successful in changing unhealthy behaviors, particularly those against smoking. Over time, these efforts can lead to greater awareness of the negative effects of smoking, thus leading to attitude change, and even behavior change. Therefore, stronger effort should go into the design and dissemination of well-targeted antismoking campaigns to further facilitate the decline in smoking among youth. Campaigns emphasizing peer pressure, family influences, and the high (monetary) price of smoking might prove to be relevant and meaningful to potential teen smokers. If emphasis is placed on limiting cigarette advertising in consumer magazines at the expense of developing effective antismoking programs, for example, this study suggests that a reduction in magazine advertising of cigarettes will have little effect on the decline of teen smoking.

Although teen smoking still remains a problem, the number of teenagers who smoke has continued to decline, at least in small part because of state-created programs designed to encourage youth not to smoke. Although cigarette advertising in consumer magazines is often cited as a primary influence on teen smoking, the results of this study indicate that these advertisements may not have the strong impact that previous research has suggested. If teen smoking is to continue its decline, emphasis on defining its cause should not be placed solely on cigarette advertising, but should also attempt to evaluate the impact of antismoking campaigns, peer influence, and parental influence on young people's decision to smoke.

> "*Exposure to movie smoking has such a considerable impact on adolescent smoking . . . because it is a very strong social influence on kids.*"

# Movies Glamorize Smoking

### *Dartmouth Medical School*

*In the following viewpoint researchers from Dartmouth Medical School assert that exposure to smoking in movies strongly influences the initiation of smoking among youths. Adolescents who are most frequently exposed to movie smoking are more than twice as likely to smoke as youths with minimal exposure, the school contends. It also claims that the impact of movie smoking is greater than the influence of peers and parents on the decision of an adolescent to try smoking. Moreover, according to the researchers, more than one-third of the adolescents studied began smoking due to exposure to movie smoking. Since 2000 the Dartmouth research team has studied the relationships between adolescent behavior and exposure to movie portrayals of smoking.*

As you read, consider the following questions:

"Adolescents Who Watch Smoking in Movies are More Likely to Try Smoking," dms.dartmouth.edu, November 7, 2005. Reproduced by permission.

1. According to the authors, what percentage of movies available to adolescents contain examples of smoking?

2. What is the relationship between ethnic and minority populations and movie smoking, according to the Dartmouth researchers?

3. What do the Dartmouth researchers suggest as ways to reduce the exposure of youths to movie smoking?

The first national study to look at the connection between smoking in movies and smoking initiation among adolescents shows that exposure to smoking in popular films is a primary risk factor in determining whether young people will start smoking.

The study by researchers from Dartmouth Medical School (DMS) and Norris Cotton Cancer Center (NCCC) appears in the November 7 [2005] issues of the journal, *Pediatrics*. The research, supported by the National Cancer Institute, suggests that exposure to movie smoking accounts for smoking initiation among over one-third of U.S. adolescents. It concludes that limiting exposure of young adolescents to movie smoking could have important public health implications.

"We found that as the amount of exposure to smoking in movies increased, the rate of smoking also increased," said lead author Dr. James Sargent, professor of pediatrics at DMS and director of the Cancer Control Research Program at NCCC. "Part of the reason that exposure to movie smoking has such a considerable impact on adolescent smoking is because it is a very strong social influence on kids ages 10–14," he said. "Because movie exposure to smoking is so pervasive, its impact on this age group outweighs whether peers or parents smoke or whether the child is involved in other activities, like sports."

In the study, 6,522 U.S. adolescents aged 10–14 were asked to identify films they had seen from a list of 50 randomly selected titles out of a database of films released in the U.S.

## Movie Smoking Lures Teens

Parents who monitor their child's movie choices are usually thinking language, violence, and sex. But a survey of nearly 5,000 middle-school students in New Hampshire and Vermont suggests that parents should also be watching for the role tobacco plays in the film.

Students who had seen more films in which smoking was depicted as cool, sexy, or otherwise positive, were more likely to try cigarettes themselves, wrote the authors of a study reported in the *British Medical Journal*.

American Cancer Society News, *January 8, 2002. www.cancer.org.*

from 1998–2000. Researchers found examples of movie smoking in 74 percent of the 532 movies in the database. Based on the movies each participant had seen and the amount of smoking in each movie, the adolescents were split into four levels of exposure to movie smoking. Researchers then examined risk for adolescent smoking, comparing adolescents in the higher movie smoking categories with the lowest category and controlling factors known to be linked with adolescent smoking, like peer and parent smoking. Even after considering all other factors known to influence the smoking risk, DMS researchers found that adolescents with the highest exposure to movie smoking were 2.6 times more likely to take up smoking compared to those with the lowest exposure. All else being equal, the researchers found that of 100 adolescents that tried smoking, 38 did so because of their exposure to smoking in movies.

The study confirms the results of a regionalized study by the researchers that focused on adolescents in Northern New England, published December 15 in the *British Medical Journal*.

The data in that research showed that exposure to smoking in movies had a similar impact on first-time cigarette smoking, but the children interviewed for that study were predominantly Caucasians living in mostly rural areas, and so the results could not be applied to the rest of the country.

"This is an extremely powerful confirmatory study that shows that kids react the same way to the movies in other places in the U.S. as they do in New England," said Sargent. "It means that no child is immune to the influence of smoking in movies."

The participants' ethnicity was taken into account as well. This large national research sample found that Hispanic and black youths were exposed to significantly more movie smoking than their white counterparts, so the population impact may be larger in minorities.

"The finding on minorities is concerning," said co-author of the study, Dr. Linda Titus-Ernstoff, professor of community and family medicine at DMS. "On average, Hispanic and black adolescents are exposed to more movie smoking than whites, so movie smoking may have a greater impact in these populations."

In the study, the researchers suggest several ways to reduce teens' exposure to movie smoking. "As a pediatrician, I think that parents need to become more aware of what their young children watch and make an effort to shield young children from the messages in PG-13 and R rated movies," said Sargent.

The team also hopes that, in light of their new research, the movie industry will be persuaded to voluntarily reduce depictions of smoking and cigarette brands. They also suggest that the movie industry could incorporate smoking into the movie rating system to make parents aware of the risks a movie with smoking poses to the adolescent viewer, and include an antismoking preview on all DVD movies that depict smoking. "Those measures would have a minimal cost to the movie industry," said Sargent.

VIEWPOINT 4

> *"Most investigators have concluded that smoking is portrayed as glamorous ... but our study shows that the exact opposite is true."*

# Movies Do Not Glamorize Smoking

## Jacob Sullum

*In the following viewpoint columnist Jacob Sullum asserts that movies do not encourage teens to smoke by glamorizing cigarettes and their use. He points out that in fact movies often depict smoking as dangerous, and he notes that "bad guys" are seen smoking more than are "good guys." Sullum also argues that life factors outweigh cinematic portrayals of smoking in influencing youths to start the habit.*

As you read, consider the following questions:

1. How do the findings of the study published in *Chest* contradict claims that smoking is glamorized in movies, according to the author?

2. What does Sullum have to say about the attempt of the

Jacob Sullum, "Flicks and Ashes," *The Washington Times*, August 23, 2005. Copyright © 2005 News World Communications, Inc. Reprinted with permission of Creators Syndicate.

"Smoke Free Movies" campaign to associate the smoking behavior of teens with their exposure to smoking scenes in movies?

3. According to Sullum, why should filmmakers reject attempts by antismoking advocates to cast them in the role of public health guardians?

In the 2005 movie "The Jacket," Kelly Lynch plays a drunk who burns to death after falling asleep while smoking. According to the research cited by activists who object to cinematic portrayals of smoking, Miss Lynch's character is part of an insidious plot to lure children into the habit by making it seem cool and glamorous.

Studies in this area typically define pro-tobacco messages broadly enough to include all instances of smoking, actual or implied, along with discussions of tobacco and glimpses of cigarette logos, lighters or ashtrays. A new study that takes a more discriminating approach, looking at the behavior of the leading characters in 447 popular films released since 1990, contradicts several claims made by critics who blame movies for encouraging kids to smoke.

## Smoking Is Not Portrayed as Glamorous

Anti-smoking activists assert that smoking is more common in movies than it is in real life. The new study, reported in the August [2005] issue of the journal *Chest* found that, overall, "contemporary American movies do not have a higher prevalence of smoking than the general U.S. population."

Activists complain that movies put cigarettes in the hands of attractive protagonists and link smoking to success and affluence. The *Chest* study found that "bad guys" were more likely to smoke than "good guys" and that, as in real life, smoking was associated with lower socioeconomic status.

"Most investigators have concluded that smoking is portrayed as glamorous and positive, but our study shows that the exact opposite is true." said lead author Karan Omidvari, a physician at St. Michael's Medical Center in Newark, N.J. Likewise, there was no evidence to support the idea that movie studios conspire with tobacco companies to target women or minorities.

Having shown that the indictment of Hollywood for pushing cigarettes is based largely on weak studies and loose talk, Dr. Omidvari and his colleagues were quick to say they nevertheless object to smoking in movies. Robert McCaffree, president of the foundation that publishes *Chest* said, "this study . . . emphasizes the need for change in this area, including increasing antitobacco messages in coming attractions and films."

## Rate Movies "R" for Smoking?

Stanton Glantz, an anti-smoking activist who was involved in much of the research debunked by Dr. Omidvari's study, has a different solution in mind: a mandatory R rating for movies that include smoking. Last fall his Smoke Free Movies campaign took out full-page ads in the *New York Times* and other publications claiming that adopting this policy "would cut movie smoking's effect on kids in half, saving 50,000 lives a year in the U.S. alone."

It's hard to say how many teenagers would be deterred by greater use of the R rating—especially if their parents knew that a single smoking scene was enough to qualify an otherwise unobjectionable movie for the not-without-a-parent-or-guardian category. But the weakest link in the chain of reasoning that charges the Motion Picture Association of America with killing 137 (middle-aged or elderly) "kids" a day by failing to make this simple change in its rating system is the assumption that half of the teenagers who start smoking do so because they saw it in the movies.

That assumption is based on a 2003 study that found 10- to 14-year-olds who had seen movies with many smoking

## An Actor and Director Speaks Out

The films we directors create tell the story of people's lives, be they in the present or the past, in our country or in a foreign culture. In telling our stories—and creating accurate depictions of life on a reel of film—filmmakers seek to capture not only who we are but also who we want to be. Directors may not always hit the mark with every film, but through the revelation of joy and pain, bravery and fear, greatness and weakness, happiness and sadness, we try to seek the truth in the story we are telling. . . . Smoking is one of the facts of real life that directors face. Without denying all the indisputable evidence that shows what smoking does to your health, the reality is that people smoke in real life. Like most personal traits, smoking can be an important signal that reveals or underscores the emotional or mental state of a character. In other instances, portraying smoking on the screen may be unavoidable if we are to establish historical accuracy. You can't portray either Roosevelts accurately without a cigar or cigarette, nor great geniuses like Einstein. The decision to smoke is one exercised by the individual director as they shape the story of their film.

*LeVar Burton, testimony before the*
*U.S. Senate Committee on Commerce,*
*Science, and Transportation, May 2004. www.dga.org.*

scenes were more likely to try cigarettes than kids who had seen movies with fewer smoking scenes. The problem with attributing this association to the modeling effect of cinematic smoking is that it's impossible to control for all the differences in personality and environment that make kids more likely to see movies with a lot of smoking in them, which tend to be R-rated movies.

Methodological difficulties aside, the size of this alleged effect is implausibly large, to put it mildly. Mr. Glantz says cinematic smoking accounts for even more real-life smoking than advertising does: 52 percent vs. 34 percent. Is it even conceivable that exposure to movies and advertising causes 86 percent of smoking? That all other factors in life together contribute only 14 percent?

At least as offensive as such patently absurd claims is the premise that every filmmaker should make his work conform to the dictates of the health nannies. Dr. Omidvari and his colleagues found that smoking was especially common in independent films, a fact they said may be due to the "antiestablishment or free-spirited" character of such movies. If anyone is making smoking seem cool, it's self-righteous busybodies like Stanton Glantz.

"*[Seventy-three percent] of the public believes that 'alcohol advertising is a major contributor to underage drinking.'*"

# Alcohol Ads Promote Underage Drinking

## *Center on Alcohol Marketing and Youth*

*In the following viewpoint the Center on Alcohol Marketing and Youth (CAMY) asserts that alcohol advertising influences youth drinking behavior. Citing statistics from multiple studies conducted throughout the United States over several years, CAMY contends that there is ample evidence that alcohol ads encourage teen drinking. The organization also maintains that alcohol advertisers target teens by producing ads that entertain and make alcohol use seem appealing. The Center on Alcohol Marketing and Youth at Georgetown University monitors the alcohol industry's marketing practices, focusing attention on actions that threaten the health and safety of youth.*

As you read, consider the following questions:

1. According to CAMY, what is the relationship between the number of ads in a magazine and its youth readership numbers?

2. What does CAMY assert about the link between exposure to (and enjoyment of) alcohol advertising and subsequent drinking behavior among teens?

3. According to the author, what is the likelihood that teens will be exposed to general alcohol ads as compared to their likely exposure to antidrinking messages targeted at them?

Research clearly indicates that, in addition to parents and peers, alcohol advertising and marketing have a significant impact on youth decisions to drink.

> While many factors may influence an underage person's drinking decisions, including among other things, parents, peers and the media, there is reason to believe that advertising also plays a role. (Federal Trade Commission, Self-Regulation in the Alcohol Industry, 1999)

Parents and peers have a large impact on youth decisions to drink. However, research clearly indicates that alcohol advertising and marketing also have a significant impact by influencing the attitudes of parents and peers and helping to create an environment that promotes underage drinking.

## How Alcohol Ads Influence Teens

- A study on alcohol advertising in magazines from 1997 to 2001 found that the number of beer and distilled spirits ads tended to increase with a magazine's youth readership. For every 1 million underage readers ages 12–19 in a magazine, researchers generally found 1.6 times more beer advertisements and 1.3 times more distilled spirits advertisements.

• A recent study of eighth-graders showed that those with greater exposure to alcohol advertisements in magazines, on television, and at sporting and music events were more aware of the advertising and more likely to remember the advertisements they had seen.

• A study of 12-year-olds found that children who were more aware of beer advertising held more favorable views on drinking and expressed an intention to drink more often as adults than did children who were less knowledgeable about the ads.

• A federally-funded study of 1,000 young people found that exposure to and liking of alcohol advertisements affects whether young people will drink alcohol.

• Another study found that, among a group of 2,250 middle-school students, those who viewed more television programs containing alcohol commercials while in the seventh grade were more likely in the eighth grade to drink beer, wine/liquor, or to drink three or more drinks on at least one occasion during the month prior to the follow-up survey.

## Should Ads Be Banned?

• A recent economic analysis assessed the effects of alcohol advertising on youth drinking behaviors by comparing federally reported levels of youth drinking with detailed reports on alcohol advertising in local markets during the same years. The analysis concluded that a complete ban on alcohol advertising could reduce monthly levels of youth drinking by 24% and youth binge drinking by about 42%.

• A 1996 study of children ages nine to 11 found that children were more familiar with Budweiser's television frogs than Kellogg's Tony the Tiger, the Mighty Morphin' Power Rangers, or Smokey the Bear.

## Youth Magazines and Alcohol Advertising

Magazines with Disproportionately High Youth Readerships with More Than a Million Dollars in Alcoholic Beverage Advertising, 2003

| Publication | Alcohol Ads | Alcohol Ad Dollars | Youth Audience Composition |
|---|---|---|---|
| Sports Illustrated | 148 | $41,122,774 | 23.2% |
| Maxim | 124 | $21,102,190 | 23.8% |
| Cosmopolitan | 68 | $11,651,335 | 21.5% |
| Rolling Stone | 112 | $11,411,660 | 29.7% |
| Entertainment Weekly | 94 | $10,094,246 | 19.2% |
| ESPN The Magazine | 73 | $9,663,300 | 31.3% |
| Stuff | 112 | $8,913,300 | 19.3% |
| FHM Magazine | 115 | $7,975,595 | 17.6% |
| Vibe | 81 | $6,484,837 | 38.9% |
| Vogue | 43 | $6,330,604 | 21.3% |
| In Style | 67 | $6,254,500 | 19.6% |
| Us Weekly | 67 | $5,327,065 | 16.8% |
| Marie Claire | 30 | $2,609,510 | 23.8% |
| Sporting News | 71 | $2,520,849 | 25.3% |
| Spin | 48 | $2,360,273 | 35.1% |
| Premiere | 43 | $2,018,136 | 23.2% |
| Jane | 33 | $1,973,243 | 18.7% |
| Glamour | 8 | $1,573,563 | 21.7% |
| Popular Mechanics | 15 | $1,529,918 | 18.2% |
| Ebony | 25 | $1,373,801 | 21.3% |
| Self | 12 | $1,125,885 | 17.7% |

Center on Alcohol Marketing and Youth, Youth Overexposed: Alcohol Advertising in Magazines, 2001 to 2003, 2005.

- The Center on Alcohol Marketing and Youth found that, from 2001 though 2003, youth in the United States were 96 times more likely per capita to see an ad promoting alcohol than an industry ad discounting underage drinking. In fact, compared to underage youth, adults age 21 and over were nearly twice as likely per capita to see advertising discouraging underage drinking.

- A *USA Today* survey found that teens say ads have a greater influence on their desire to drink in general than on their desire to buy a particular brand of alcohol.

- Eighty percent of general public respondents in a poll by the Bureau of Alcohol, Tobacco and Firearms believed "that alcohol advertising influences youth to drink alcoholic beverages." Another poll, done for an alcohol-industry-funded organization called the Century Council, found that 73% of the public believes that "alcohol advertising is a major contributor to underage drinking."

- The National Association of Broadcasters (NAB) recognizes the influence advertising can have on youth: "[T]he impact of advertising on radio and television audiences, particularly kids, cannot be overstated. Clever jingles, flashy lights, fast talking, and quick pacing, all contribute to the message of commercials."

- $1.79 billion was spent on alcohol advertising in measured media (television, radio, print, outdoor, major newspapers and Sunday supplements) in 2003. Working from alcohol company documents submitted to them, the Federal Trade Commission estimated in 1999 that the alcohol industry's total expenditures to promote alcohol (including through sponsorship, Internet advertising, point-of-sale materials, product placement, brand-logoed items and other means) were three or more times its expenditures for measured media advertising. This would mean that the alcohol industry spent a total of $5.37 billion or more on advertising and promotion in 2003.

| "The purpose of ads for alcoholic beverages . . . is to encourage brand shifting, not to convert non-drinkers into drinkers."

# Alcohol Ads Do Not Promote Underage Drinking

*Robert A. Levy*

*Robert A. Levy is a senior fellow in constitutional studies at the Cato Institute, a libertarian think tank. In this viewpoint he contends that alcohol ads are not targeted to teens nor are they designed to convince nondrinkers to start consuming alcohol. On the contrary, Levy argues, alcohol advertising is designed to convince consumers to switch brands. Levy also asserts that there is little evidence that alcohol ads influence underage drinking.*

As you read, consider the following questions:

1. What is the general attitude of the author toward allowing the legal system to control the advertising practices of private companies promoting legal goods?
2. According to the Federal Trade Commission's 2003

examination of alcohol ads, as cited by Levy, what is the stated purpose of such ads?

3. How does the author characterize the choice between regulation of alcohol ads and preserving core First Amendment values?

Hardly a week passes without a reminder that the state tobacco lawsuits have had an enduring and corrupting effect on the rule of law. The legal travesty du jour involves yet another "sin" industry. This time the trial lawyers are hounding the purveyors of alcoholic beverages because of ads ostensibly targeted, "deliberately and recklessly," at underage consumers.

## The Lawsuits

Here's the cast of characters: The plaintiffs are a class of parents and guardians of kids too young to drink but exposed to the ads. Representing the class are a pair of law firms: one headed by David Boies, the eminent litigator hired by the U.S. Justice Department to go after Microsoft; and a second headed by his son, David Boies III. The defendants include the Beer Institute and a number of large distillers and brewers such as Coors, Heineken and Brown-Forman. Interestingly, the two largest domestic beer producers, Anheuser-Busch and Miller, clients of Boies senior, are not among the defendants.

Supposedly, the offending companies advertise in magazines "disproportionately read" by young people, place their products in movies seen by teens, make their Web sites accessible to minors, allude to college activities like "spring break," and use cartoon characters—probably the same way MetLife uses Snoopy to hoodwink all those gullible adolescents into buying insurance policies.

Never mind that our drinking laws are absurd. An 18-year-old is presumably mature enough to sign contracts, get married, have an abortion, go to war and decide who is going to run the country. But he's three years away from coping with the weighty implications of consuming a can of beer. Nor can a person of age 20, according to the Boies team, possibly resist the allure of a movie star enjoying a brew in a PG-13 film. In the end, how does a brewer or distiller, or a jury for that matter, distinguish an ad that would be suitable for a 21-year-old from an ad that might be construed as impermissibly "targeted" at a 20-year-old?

## Analysis Finds Teens Are Not Targeted by Alcohol Ads

It's not as if this issue has escaped scrutiny. The Federal Trade Commission's 2003 Report on Alcohol Marketing and Advertising, approved by the commission without dissent, looked at nine major companies and analyzed their ads, marketing plans and consumer research. The report "found no evidence of targeting underage consumers" in the increasingly popular market for flavored malt beverages, which combine beer and distilled spirits. The purpose of ads for alcoholic beverages, like ads for vehicles, is to encourage brand shifting, not to convert non-drinkers into drinkers.

There's another key concern when courts are asked to enjoin private companies from exercising their commercial speech rights. In a 1983 case, *Bolger vs. Youngs Drug Prods. Corp.*, the U.S. Supreme Court remarked that government must not "reduce the adult population . . . to reading only what is fit for children." Then, 13 years later, the court held that even "vice" products like alcoholic beverages are entitled to commercial speech protection (*44 Liquormart Inc. vs. Rhode Island*). Indeed, our Constitution protects Ku Klux Klan speech, flag burning and gangsta rap, which is targeted directly at teenagers. Yet if Coors wants to advertise Keystone Light in *Sports Illustrated*, Boies and his team of lawyers would bring the boot of government down hard on the company's neck.

## The Federal Trade Commission Weighs In

At the request of Congress, the Federal Trade Commission (FTC) carefully investigated whether or not flavored malt beverages (FMBs) or malternatives are being marketed to persons under the age of 21.

The FTC, in cooperation with the Bureau of Alcohol, Tobacco and Firearms (BATF), conducted an exhaustive analysis of internal company documents on product development, marketing strategies, advertising strategies, age composition of FMB ads, among many other matters. It also conducted a study of the actual placement of FMBs in retail locations across the country. In addition, the FTC consulted with and received information from alcohol activist groups such as the Center for Science in the Public Interest's Alcohol Policies Project (CSPI), the Center on Alcohol Marketing and Youth (CAMY), and Mothers Against Drunk Driving (MADD).

The FTC "found no evidence of targeting underage drinkers in the FMB market" and it noted that "the majority of FMB drinkers are over the age of 27," much higher than the minimum drinking age. It also observed that "teen drinking continued to decline during the period when these beverages were being aggressively marketed."

David J. Hanson, "Do Alcohol Ads Target Youth?" Alcohol Problems and Solutions, 2005.

However serious the problem of underage consumption of beer and liquor, there are countervailing values that are implicated when speech restrictions are proposed.

The choice between preserving core 1st Amendment values and regulating ads for alcoholic beverages is a particularly easy one when there is little evidence of any connection between those ads and underage drinking. We need not sacrifice commercial free speech to reduce alcohol consumption by minors. Nor should we sit back and allow the trial lawyers to add one more notch to their expanding tobacco belt. Their message is simple: The doctrine of personal accountability is out the window. In its place is the insidious notion that you can engage in risky behavior, then force someone else to pay for your mistakes. That message is far more pernicious than any beer or liquor commercial.

# Periodical Bibliography

The following articles have been selected to supplement the diverse views presented in this chapter.

Edward W. Boyer "The Internet and Psychoactive Substance Use Among Innovative Drug Users," *Pediatrics*, February 2005.

Jules Crittenden "Big-Screen Boozing May Lure Middle School Kids to Drink," *Boston Herald*, May 26, 2004.

Becky Ebenkamp "Sex, Drugs & R'n'R High School," *Brandweek*, September 5, 2005.

Stanton A. Glantz "Smoking in Movies: A Major Problem and a Real Solution," *Lancet*, July 26, 2003.

Linda Haugstead "Liquor Ads Influence the Young," *Multichannel News*, December 19, 2005.

Alyse R. Lancaster "Teenage Exposure to Cigarette Advertising in Popular Consumer Magazines: Vehicle Versus Message Reach and Frequency," *Journal of Advertising*, Fall 2003.

Karl E. Miller "Adolescent Exposure to Magazine Alcohol Advertising," *American Family Physician*, May 1, 2005.

Jon P. Nelson "Advertising, Alcohol, and Youth: Is the Alcoholic Beverage Industry Targeting Minors with Magazine Ads?" *Regulation*, Summer 2005.

OPPOSING
VIEWPOINTS®
SERIES

# CHAPTER 4

# How Can Teen Drug Abuse Be Prevented?

# Chapter Preface

Increasing evidence indicates that teens with strong family ties and a sense of personal connection to school personnel and activities are less likely to smoke, drink, or use drugs than are teens whose family and school ties are weak. Since the National Longitudinal Study of Adolescent Health (NLSAH) first documented this correlation in 1997, drug use prevention programs have developed ways to increase teens' ties with families and schools as the centerpiece of their educational efforts. One of the best-known campaigns is the slogan, "Parents: The Anti-Drug." This slogan, familiar from television and print ads, originated with the White House Office of National Drug Control Policy (ONDCP). Critics of such antidrug advertising and public service announcements suggest that they oversimplify the NLSAH's findings, and ignore the underlying details of the research.

Before examining the critics' claims, it is important to clarify what the NLSAH found. The researchers claim that the presence of drugs, alcohol, and tobacco products in a teen's home increases the likelihood that youths will use these substances. In contrast, the study also found that the presence of a parent at key points during a teen's day decreases the likelihood of teen drug use. Moreover, teens who feel valued at school, both among peers and among teachers, were discovered to be less likely to abuse alcohol or drugs.

Prevention programs that rely on ad campaigns and slogans such as "Parents: The Anti-Drug," tend to miss the point of the NLSAH's results, say critics. Even though there may be a connection between abstinence and teens' strong ties with adults, it does not follow that such ties can be forged through sound-bites, critics assert. According to a survey co-published in 2002 by the research firm Westat and the University of Pennsylvania, teens' attitudes and drug-use behaviors were not significantly affected by a five-year, $900 million antidrug ad campaign mounted by the ONDCP. In fact, some survey responses suggest that older teens are simply amused by the efforts and that younger viewers are slightly more willing to try certain drugs after seeing the ads. About the preventative value of antidrug advertising campaigns, Ed Spitsbergen, a drug and alcohol counselor for teens at Growth Works counseling center in Plymouth, Michigan, offers this observation: "It may work for some. . . . But we have adults who are using drugs and alcohol on a pretty regular basis. And kids basically are going to do what adults do." To experts such as Spitzbergen, no slogan can create the kinds of connections that tend to decrease teen drug use or mitigate the factors that lead to substance abuse.

The critics have not yet won the debate, however. Tom Riley, spokesperson for the ONDCP, stands by prevention efforts of all kinds, including the use of public service announcements. He says, "If you don't start using drugs by the time you're 20, you're never going to do drugs. If you don't start using drugs as a teenager, you're never going to become an addict. . . . If you can just prevent kids from starting, it's by far the best investment." The viewpoints in the following chapter debate the benefits and drawbacks of popular drug use prevention and education efforts. As in the case of public service announcements warning about the dangers of drugs, the approaches explored are highly controversial.

*"Student drug testing is
a deterrent."*

# Drug Testing Can Deter Teen Drug Use

*Calvina L. Fay*

*Calvina L. Fay is the executive director of the Drug Free America Foundation, which focuses on developing and promoting strategies, policies, and laws to reduce illegal drug use. In the following viewpoint she advocates student drug testing as a deterrent to teen drug use. She asserts that drug testing in schools is a useful tool for identifying drug problems and referring students and their families to treatment programs. She maintains that student drug testing is neither inaccurate, as charged by critics, nor an invasion of students' privacy.*

As you read, consider the following questions:

1. What are the benefits of drug testing for students and their families, as identified by Fay?
2. According to the author, what misconceptions exist about student drug testing?

Calvina L. Fay, "Student Drug Testing Is Part of the Solution," *Behavioral Health Management*, vol. 24, July August 2004, p. 13. Copyright 2004 Medquest Communications. Reproduced by permission.

3. In the opinion of the author, what is the one drawback
to current standards for student drug testing, as allowed
by the federal government?

In his 2004 State of the Union address, President [George
W.] Bush not only endorsed student drug testing, but he
asked for $23 million in additional government funds to
implement such programs nationwide. For those in the drug
abuse prevention field, this decision was paradigmatic, a firm
description of what should be. Although some feel student
drug testing is invasive, there is no denying it is an effective
tool for identifying and preventing drug problems.

The intent of such programs is not to punish students.
The goals are to deter drug use and for the drug user to
straighten out his or her life. The results are not turned over
to law enforcement; rather, they are discussed with the parents
of the child in question so, as a family, they can discuss which
type of drug treatment is suitable for their child. Drug use affects cognitive abilities and attention span, making it difficult
for the user to properly learn and succeed in school. The
benefits of student drug testing in addressing this abound.

School drug testing, as implemented today, applies only to
students who voluntarily choose to participate in athletic and
extracurricular activities. Student athletes and students in
extracurricular activities take leadership roles in the school
community and, as role models, should be drug-free—and
student drug testing helps ensure this. More importantly, it
gives students in extracurricular activities an "out" or an argument that they can use with drug-using peers when pressured
to take drugs (e.g., "If I take drugs, the coach will know
because I have to take a drug test, and then I'll be kicked off
the team"). Today, drug testing is a standard procedure when
applying for a job. Certainly, athletes who want to compete at
the collegiate or Olympic level should get used to the idea of
drug testing.

## Misconceptions About Drug Testing

Some people criticize drug testing on grounds it can be inaccurate. This charge is incorrect. The drug-testing procedures in place today eliminate the possibility of a false positive. If schools follow drug-testing procedures recommended by the White House Office of National Drug Control Policy, students will provide a urine specimen in a private rest-room area. The specimen will be handled under the chain of custody guidelines, a set of procedures to account for the integrity of each urine specimen by tracking its handling and storage from collection to disposition of the specimen. If the screening test is positive, confirmation is sought with a more sensitive test. If the confirmation test is positive, a physician trained in drug testing then reviews it and contacts the student to see if there is a legitimate medical reason for the positive result. Drug test results are confidential, and federal law prevents them from being released outside the school. And the results do not follow the student once he or she leaves high school (as per the Family Educational Rights and Privacy Act).

Another misconception about student drug testing is that it is expensive and difficult to implement. A drug test costs only between $10 and 30 per student, a cost that is nominal compared to its true worth. Any school that receives federal education funding is permitted to use these funds for drug testing; the No Child Left Behind Act specifically authorizes the expenditure of federal education funds for student drug testing. So, if the money is there, let's put it to good use.

I have worked with many like-minded individuals on this issue who all agree that student drug testing is a deterrent although effective only when coupled with other drug-prevention and education initiatives. Along these lines, attorney David Evans is making many important strides with the Drug-Free Schools Coalition in New Jersey. Evans stresses an important point when he says, "Many schools find great value in using random drug and alcohol testing [for student

## Student Drug Testing Is Not a Privacy Issue

There are those who represent student drug testing as a tool of "Big Brother" and a violation of personal privacy. Upon examination, these concerns have turned out to be largely unfounded and often exaggerated. The Supreme Court, in fact, carefully weighed the privacy issue, ultimately determining that a school's interest in protecting children from the influence of drugs outweighs their expectation of privacy. The court further mandated that the results of the tests be kept confidential—shared only with the parents of the student, in order to help refer the student into the appropriate level of counseling or treatment, not punishment.

*John P. Walters, "Random Student Drug Testing Works," Post-Gazette.com, 2005. www.post-gazette.com.*

athletes and those in extracurricular activities] as part of their antidrug programs. The goal of drug testing is to deter drug and alcohol use. Students who know they may be detected are less likely to use drugs or alcohol, not to mention experience the consequences of addiction."

## Only Some Students May Be Tested

The unfortunate part of student drug testing today is that we cannot test those who do not participate in extracurricular activities. These students encounter the same peer pressure that the extracurricular students face, but they don't have the same drug-testing defense, making it potentially more difficult to say no to drugs. Although schools that test athletes and students in other extracurricular activities experience an overall decline in drug use, they must not forget about those students who do not benefit from drug testing and at least provide them with other drug prevention and education alternatives.

As a drug-policy and prevention expert with more than 20 years' experience, I have fought for this issue alongside many parents who have lost their children to drugs. These parents have told me time and time again, "I never suspected that my child was using drugs. If I had only known, I could have done something." It kills me every time I hear this. Student drug testing is one of the best ways to identify a problem and offer a chance for parents to know about it and get help before it is too late.

| *"It is fairly easy to fool drug tests, and . . . most drug-involved youth are all too familiar with ways to do so."*

# Drug Testing Does Not Deter Teen Drug Use

### John R. Knight and Sharon Levy

*John R. Knight is the director of the Center for Adolescent Substance Abuse Research, and Sharon Levy is the director of pediatrics at Children's Hospital in Boston. In this viewpoint they argue that student drug testing is ineffective because teens find ways to falsify urine samples. The authors also express concern that students will shift from using fairly safe drugs such as marijuana, which is detected by the tests, to more dangerous drugs such as inhalants, which are not tested for. Moreover, Knight and Levy maintain, these tests violate students' privacy rights.*

As you read, consider the following questions:

1. How is the validity of urine samples ensured, according to the authors?

John R. Knight and Sharon Levy, "An F for School Drug Tests," *Boston Globe*, June 12, 2005. © Copyright 2005 Globe Newspaper Company. Reproduced by permission of the authors.

2. As related by Knight and Levy, what substances are most abused by teens?

3. What percentage of students at Massachusetts high schools had used marijuana during the previous thirty days, as cited by the authors?

Lieutenant Governor [of Massachusetts] Kerry Healy unveiled a plan [in 2005] to identify teens with drug problems through high school drug testing programs, which were ruled legal by the United States Supreme Court in 2002. The Bush administration has also been a proponent of high school drug testing, and has set aside millions of dollars in federal assistance for local school districts. Dr. John Walters, the director of the President's Office of National Drug Control Policy, has previously described drug testing in schools as a "silver bullet" solution to the epidemic of substance abuse among our youth.

We are in favor of any approach that helps, but we disagree with the widespread implementation of high school drug testing programs for a number of reasons. First, we are skeptical that any single public policy will solve this complex problem.

We also believe that implementation of drug testing should await scientific evidence that it is both safe and effective—and we have neither. Laboratory testing for drugs is an invasive and complex procedure.

In order to ensure the validity of the specimen, urination must either be directly observed—an embarrassing procedure for all—or the collector must use a protocol that includes temperature testing, controls for adulteration and dilution, and documentation of a continuous chain of custody in handling. In a recent national survey we found that very few physicians have the expertise to collect specimens properly, and we doubt that most schools have staff that can. Without proper controls, students can easily falsify urine samples. Even when proper collection procedures are used, it is fairly easy to

Steve Kelley. © 1989 Steve Kelley, *The San Diego Union-Tribune*. Reprinted with permission.

fool drug tests, and our clinical experience indicates that most drug-involved youth are all too familiar with ways to do so. One need only browse the Internet to see the array of products whose sole purpose is to thwart the validity of drug tests.

## Unintended Consequences

Even when properly collected, drug tests yield very limited information. With the exception of marijuana, the window of detection for most drugs is less than 48 hours.

Therefore, negative tests tell us only that the student did not use a drug during the past two days. Standard drug testing panels also do not detect many of the drugs most frequently abused by teens, such as alcohol, Ecstasy (MDMA), OxyContin, and inhalants.

Indeed, we have worked with many teens whose early drug use was missed because negative drug tests gave parents and physicians a false sense of reassurance. Furthermore, we are concerned that widespread implementation of drug testing may inadvertently encourage students to use more alcohol.

It may also motivate drug-involved teens to move from drugs that are less dangerous, such as marijuana, to those that are more dangerous but not detected by the test.

We are also concerned about the effects of this potential invasion of an adolescent's privacy.

Some students will sit in class studying our constitutional protection against unreasonable search and seizure and then be compelled to produce a urine specimen against their will. What is the lesson here? For many of these same reasons, the American Academy of Pediatrics has taken a stand against drug testing of adolescents as a screening procedure, and we support that decision.

Drug testing is best employed as a routine component of a drug treatment program to ensure maintenance of abstinence. Lastly, while we are encouraged that the current plan would provide money to cities and towns for substance abuse counseling, we are concerned that funds will not meet the current need for adolescent drug treatment.

A recent survey of Massachusetts high school students revealed that more than 30 percent had used marijuana during the past 30 days. What will happen to those students who test positive?

We applaud Lieutenant Governor Healy for insisting that the focus of drug testing should be on helping kids find treatment—and not punishing them—but it is largely an empty promise.

As pediatricians, we are confronted daily with the lack of developmentally appropriate substance abuse treatment for teenagers in Massachusetts. We often must choose between no treatment and placing youth in adult substance abuse treatment programs, which is often ineffective.

School drug testing programs will be very costly.

While they are increasing in popularity, their efficacy is unproven and they are associated with significant technical concerns.

We urge Healy and other public officials to place our scarce resources first into proven prevention, early intervention, and treatment programs for adolescents. Let us not rush to accept the illusory view that drug testing in schools is the silver bullet for the prevention of youth substance abuse.

| *"When teens are allowed to drink at home, they are more likely to use alcohol and other drugs outside the home."*

# Abstinence-Only Substance Abuse Education Is Effective

## Jay Mathews

*In the following viewpoint journalist Jay Mathews profiles a mother's effort to take a stand against the practice, popular among her own peers, of allowing underage drinking in the home. He notes that the abstinence-based guide to substance abuse that the woman wrote for the parents and teens of the Georgetown Preparatory school is grounded in science. Studies find, he claims, that teens who are allowed to drink in the home are more likely to abuse drugs later in life. Mathews asserts that an abstinence-only approach works because parents, schools, and teens work together to reduce underage drinking within the community.*

As you read, consider the following questions:

    1. According to the author, why have otherwise law-abiding

parents traditionally consented to hosting parties at which underage drinking takes place?

2. How do science-based data and illustrations contribute to the effectiveness of "A Parent's Guide for the Prevention of Alcohol, Tobacco, and Other Drug Use," according to the author?

3. As stated by Mathews, what role does parental example play in the formation of teen attitudes toward drinking?

It took Mimi Fleury a while to discover that one of the worst ideas in America is teaching your teenager to drink responsibly.

Back in 1993, when the oldest of her three sons was starting high school, she faced the demon that all parents of teenagers face: what should she do about alcohol? Friends told her: "Drinking is a rite of passage, Mimi. Let them drink in your basement, where you can keep an eye on them. Just take the car keys. If you don't teach them to drink responsibly now, they will go wild in college."

She did not take their advice. She and her plastic surgeon husband, who live in Chevy Chase, were not comfortable telling their children it was okay to break the law on underage drinking. But she still was not sure what positive action she could take.

Then James P. Power, the headmaster of her sons' school, Georgetown Preparatory in North Bethesda, talked her into producing a booklet of advice for parents on this subject as part of her role as president of the school's Parents' Board. She began calling medical authorities and checking the latest research, where she found this remarkable finding in a National Institutes of Health study: 40 percent of people who are drinking by age 15 become alcoholics at some point in their lives.

That was enough for Fleury. She and a group of other Georgetown Prep parents got to work, with help from Beth

Kane Davidson, director of Suburban Hospital's Addiction Treatment Center. Five years later, the 28-page booklet they produced has become an underground sensation, with more than 750,000 copies requested by parents and schools around the country, despite zero publicity. They call themselves the Community of Concern. They not only distribute the booklet but have used a $100,000 donation from Houston parent and builder David Weekley, to create a new tool—an online course for parents based on the booklet and designed by Baylor University experts.

## Peer Pressure for Parents, Too

And yet they still worry about parents who think that alcohol is a necessary learning experience for adolescents, like first kisses or SAT tests. The fear of offending such people was so great that in the initial version of their booklet, then thought to be just for Georgetown Prep parents, the following words— now prominently displayed on page 2—did not appear:

"'Learning how to drink' during adolescence is not a 'rite of passage' nor a 'part of growing up'. When teens are allowed to drink at home, they are more likely to use alcohol and other drugs outside the home AND are at risk to develop serious behavioral and health problems related to substance use."

Fleury said the group knew many nice, intelligent people who would be alienated immediately if that were the booklet's message. They told themselves that changing the culture was a gradual process, and they had to take small steps.

But then the calls started to pour in. Georgetown Prep parents showed the booklet to friends with children at other schools. Fleury knew there was nothing else like it, since she had searched in vain for something she could crib from when Power had pushed her to get the booklet done. But she had not expected such a growing demand for the results of her little project. Everybody seemed to want a copy, so the Georgetown Prep parents invited parents at other schools to participate in spreading the news.

## Evidence Supports Abstinence-Based Education

According to the study [by Dr. Robert Lerner, published in the Institute for Youth Development's peer-reviewed journal *Adolescent & Family Health*], released in April 2005, junior-high and middle school-aged girls who participated in the Best Friends program [promoting abstinence], when compared to their peers who did not participate, were:

- Six-and-a-half times more likely to remain abstinent;

- Nearly two times more likely to abstain from drinking alcohol;

- Eight times more likely to abstain from drug use; and

- Over two times more likely to refrain from smoking.

Melissa G. Pardue, "More Evidence of the Effectiveness of Abstinence Education Programs," The Heritage Foundation, 2005.

The previously censored warning against home schooling in beer and wine consumption went into the next edition. Once the Georgetown Prep group realized parents yearned to see the research on the effect of alcohol on adolescent brains, they no longer feared being written off as teetotalling cranks. The booklet became better, and even more popular. It says that kids should wait until their brains and bodies are both physically and emotionally mature enough to deal with the biochemical alterations of alcohol ingestion. The research indicates that people are not ready to drink until their early twenties. The law and science say the same thing independently—don't drink until 21.

Most of the Community of Concern activists are private school parents, who have begun to see that the big tuition bills they are paying don't make much sense if alcohol and other controlled substances are going to lead their kids to blow off their homework, forget their lessons and risk a rejection from their first-choice college. The booklet's professionally printed research data, including color photos and brain diagrams, cost the group $5 a copy to produce at first, but the growing volume has cut the price to $1.65. Each school must order 1,000 copies to join the group. Fleury praises the example of Georgetown Prep admissions director Michael Horsey, who holds a meeting each spring for all boys just admitted to the ninth grade, and their families, to get their copies of "A Parent's Guide for the Prevention of Alcohol, Tobacco, and Other Drug Use," and discuss its contents before the boys begin to attend the school.

## Communities Working Together

Fleury says the initiative is not just about parents helping their kids, but also parents helping other parents, schools helping other schools, communities helping other communities. "The magic lies in the idea of the partnership of parents, students and schools working together to prevent underage drinking," she said.

The school ordering the booklet gets its insignia, its substance abuse policy and a list of other participating schools in its area prominently displayed on the front or back covers. This tells parents that this is not some generic pamphlet copied off the Internet, but that their school has endorsed the contents and made it a priority. Fleury said parents have told her they love the science inside, such as an MRI of an adolescent brain showing the many areas not yet fully wired, and vulnerable to damage from too many parties, supervised or otherwise.

"In the past, you could have a discussion with another parent about whether drinking should be a rite of passage and both of you could walk away with your opinions still intact," Fleury said. "But not after you read this. You cannot argue with the scientific facts."

That doesn't mean the prevailing American cultural assumptions about alcohol have changed much, Fleury admits. That was evident when she first called me . . . and I asked her about a breaking story I was working on—the drunk driving arrest of Alexandria, Va., school superintendent Rebecca Perry. She didn't know about it. On the telephone line I heard a pause, and then a gasp. "But she signed our statement!" Fleury said.

It turned out that Perry was one of 48 educators to endorse a Community of Concern manifesto written by local education leaders. The signers promised, among other things, to model appropriate behavior for their students. Perry subsequently apologized to Alexandria students and parents for what she called a big mistake. Fleury said she was aware of Perry's statement and hoped she would continue to support the prevention of underage drinking by using the booklet in her district. An Alexandria schools spokeswoman said Perry is doing just that, with 5,500 booklets in both English and Spanish set to be distributed this year. Montgomery County [Maryland] distributed 10,000 booklets [in 2003], but lacks the funds to do more.

## Change Comes Slowly

There does not seem to be much of a sense of urgency. Some radio talk show hosts in the Washington area, and many of their callers, said they did not see why the Perry incident was such a big deal. She was a very effective superintendent, they said. She didn't kill anybody. Lots of responsible people get into that situation. There was much shrugging on the air.

As I have indicated before, I am an extremist on this issue. I got drunk twice when I was a teenager, did not like it, and have limited my alcohol intake since to one sip of wine every five years or so. I have on occasion contemplated voting for the Prohibitionist Party candidate for president, and would be happy to empty out the family liquor cabinet if my wife would let me (except for the vermouth that I need for my dynamite mustard sauce). I think one of the reasons why none of our three adult children drink is because neither my wife nor I do.

So I hope the Community of Concern someday goes one step further and suggests that parents think about curtailing their own alcohol use while they have teenagers at home. No matter what they say or don't say to their children, their example still had great power. I learned this while researching a book on our best public high schools. I visited one of the regular high school keg parties conducted in the Sheldrake Woods near a country club in Mamaroneck, N.Y. I nearly broke a leg tripping over tree roots in the dark, but eventually I found the party—several dozen teenagers, bundled up against the November chill, standing around with plastic cups of beer in their hands, making light conversation.

It looked exactly like every adult cocktail party I had ever attended. It was no mystery whose habits they were emulating, and the Community of Concern research makes clear this was just practice for the more serious drinking they would do in college—and about which they had heard their parents express such warm memories.

But that's just me. Fleury and her group seem to be moving forward carefully, gauging just how much their audience can take. It occurred to me, while reading their booklet, that I never hear parents these days say they want their children to learn to smoke responsibly. So that's progress. I hope we have more.

| "In general, 'zero tolerance' policies simply push students away."

# Abstinence-Only Substance Abuse Education Is Sometimes Ineffective

*Marsha Rosenbaum*

*Medical sociologist Marsha Rosenbaum argues in the following viewpoint that zero-tolerance and "just-say-no" education programs are not effective in protecting students from the dangers of substance abuse. She notes that abstinence-based education efforts take place within the context of a society that embraces many forms of drug use, thus the abstinence message appears hypocritical to teens. While Rosenbaum concedes that youths should be informed about the dangers of drug use and encouraged not to experiment with drugs, she also contends that students ought to be taught how to use drugs safely in the event that they do not "just say no."*

As you read, consider the following questions:

Marsha Rosenbaum, "A Reality-Based Approach to Teens and Drugs," *National Association of School Psychologists Communique*, vol. 33, December 4, 2004. Copyright 2004 by the National Association of School Psychologists, Bethesda, MD. Reprinted by permission of the publisher. www.nasponline.org.

1. According to the author, what are some of the ways in which American society specifically contradicts the "drug-free" message of many drug abuse education programs?

2. How can reality-based education and counseling protect students more effectively than abstinence-based substance abuse programs, according to the author?

3. According to Rosenbaum, how do zero-tolerance policies do more harm than good to students who are at greatest risk of substance abuse?

Like many parents, when my children entered adolescence, I wished "the drug thing" would magically disappear and my children would simply abstain. But as a drug abuse expert whose research was sponsored by the National Institute on Drug Abuse, and as a parent, I knew this wish to be a fantasy.

It comes as no surprise to school psychologists and counselors that despite federal expenditures for prevention "education" exceeding $2 billion per year (and five to seven times that at state and local levels), government surveys consistently show that half of American teenagers admit to experimenting with drugs by the time they graduate from high school, and 8 out of 10 have tried alcohol.

Today's adolescents have been exposed, since elementary school, to the most intensive and expensive anti-drug campaign in history. Haven't they been told, again and again, to "just say no" by school-based programs such as Drug Abuse Resistance Education (DARE) and hard-hitting media campaigns? Why hasn't the goal of teen abstinence been achieved? Where have we gone wrong, and what can we, as parents, counselors and school psychologists, do to ensure the safety of our teenagers?

## The Context of Prevention

As a sociologist, I believe it's important to look at the *context* of our prevention efforts. Though we urge our young people to be "drug-free," the American public, including children, are perpetually bombarded with messages that encourage them to imbibe and medicate with a variety of substances. Alcohol, tobacco, caffeine, over-the-counter and prescription drugs seem to be everywhere. In fact, the *Journal of the American Medical Association* recently reported that 80% of adults in the U.S. use at least one medication every week, and half take a prescription drug. Nearly one in two American adults uses alcohol regularly; and more than one-third have tried marijuana at some time in their lives, a fact not lost on their children.

An additional factor makes the "drug-free" mantra problematic. Today's teenagers have witnessed the increasing "Ritalinization" of their fellow (difficult-to-manage) students, and stimulants such as Adderal have become a drug of choice on college campuses. All of us have seen prime-time commercials for drugs to manage such ailments as "Generalized Anxiety Disorder," with teenagers the most recent market for anti-depressants. Teenage drug use seems to mirror modern American drug-taking tendencies. Therefore, some psychologists have argued that given the nature of our culture, to define teenage experimentation with legal and illegal substances as "deviant" is inaccurate.

A common, though faulty, assumption driving our prevention efforts is that if teenagers simply believe that experimentation with alcohol or other drugs is dangerous, they will abstain. As a result, many programs include exaggerated risk and danger messages. Although the old *Reefer Madness*-style messages have been replaced with assertions that we now have scientific "proof" that drugs are dangerous, critical evaluations, particularly of marijuana, pierce holes in the most common assertions and are inconsistent with students' observations and experiences. Hence the cynicism we see in so many teenagers regarding the anti-drug messages they regularly receive.

## Science-Based Education and School Policies

It's time to dispense with messages designed to frighten students, and replace them with drug education based on solid science that will prepare them for lifelong decisions, such as appropriate dose levels and the effect of combinations, about a range of substances they might ingest.

On the technical side, the subject could easily be integrated into a variety of high school courses and curricula, including physiology and biology (to learn how drugs affect the body), psychology (to learn how drugs affect the mind), chemistry (to learn what's contained in drugs), history and civics (to learn how drugs have been handled by the government), and social studies (to learn who uses which drugs, and why).

Even the best education isn't enough. It is important for students to have a safe place where they can talk honestly and openly, and share their fears and concerns without judgment. Many conversations about alcohol and other drugs already happen in the offices of the trusted school counselor or psychologist, or as part of a growing number of student assistance programs.

But when dealing with students who are not abstinent, who say "maybe" or "sometimes" or "yes" to alcohol and other drug use, many professionals face an impossible dilemma. They want to help, to open honest conversations, but are strapped by abstinence-only, zero tolerance policies, rendering them unable to advise those students who need them most. It's a long road from experimentation to abuse, and school psychologists, freed up from policies derived from politics rather than science, can make a real difference in keeping students safe.

*Problems with Punitive Policies* There are no easy answers when it comes to teenage use of alcohol and other drugs, but it's clear that increasingly punitive measures make the situation worse.

Random drug testing, the "silver bullet" promised and promoted by the federal government, has many pitfalls. First, the largest-ever national survey (76,000 students) to measure drug testing reported in 2003 that there is no difference in illegal drug use among students from schools with or without drug testing. Drug testing alienates students, who must be observed by a school official while urinating to be sure the sample is their own. The collection of a specimen is a humiliating violation of the most basic privacy, and especially embarrassing for an adolescent. Testing can have the unanticipated effect of keeping students from participating in extracurricular programs-activities that would fill their time during the peak teenage drug-using hours of 3–6 PM. Finally, drug testing is expensive. School administrators in Dublin, Ohio, for example, calculated that their $35,000 per year program was not cost-efficient. Of 1,473 students tested at $24 each, 11 tested positive, for a total cost of $3,200 per "positive" student. They canceled the program and, with the savings, were able to hire a full-time counselor.

In general, "zero tolerance" policies simply push students away, though research from the National Longitudinal Study of Adolescent Health shows that school connectedness has a direct relationship to lowered health risk behaviors such as drug use. That's why [in 2003] the California State PTA [Parent Teacher Association] passed a resolution to "support in-school suspension, after school interventions, positive behavior mentoring, student assistance and other programs that offer counseling and education as a preventive disciplinary response to student drug abuse." Most recently, the National Institutes of Health reported that "get tough" youth programs, as well as boot camps and DARE, are ineffective. The report cited various forms of counseling as most effective.

## Safety First Project

Similar to comprehensive sex education, reality-based drug education, coupled with counseling when needed, has the

## A Science-Based Approach to Drug Abuse Prevention

Conventional drug education programs focus predominately on abstinence-only messages and are shaped by problematic myths:

- Myth #1: Experimentation with drugs is not a common part of teenage culture;
- Myth #2: Drug use is the same as drug abuse;
- Myth #3: Marijuana is the gateway to drugs such as heroin and cocaine; and
- Myth #4: Exaggerated risks will deter young people from experimentation.

*Drug Policy Alliance, "Safety First: Parents, Teens and Drugs," 2005. www.drugpolicy.org.*

promise of increasing students' knowledge, awareness and safety.

Although parents today are strongly encouraged to have "the drug talk" with their teens, many are uncomfortable with the subject. Some don't know enough; others know too much; they're embarrassed—so the talk falls into the lap of the school psychologist or counselor. That's why the Drug Policy Alliance created the Safety First project in 1999, as a drug education program for educators and parents looking for balanced information and alternatives to failed "just say no"-style approaches, as well as ways to talk with teens about drugs. We provide free, easily digestible written materials, including the 17-page booklet, *Safety First: A Reality-Based Approach to Teens, Drugs, and Drug Education*, a take-action brochure

(*Getting Real About Teens and Drugs*), a website (www.safety1st.org) containing balanced fact sheets about a variety of drugs, a Q & A column, news and more; and a video (*Let's Talk*) of teens talking about drug education. We are now an allied agency of the California State PTA, and have distributed over 120,000 packets to parents and educators all over the world. We are pleased to make these resources available (through our website) to members of the National Association of School Psychologists.

A popular sample of our materials is a letter I wrote to my own son, published in the *San Francisco Chronicle* when he started high school. I received dozens of e-mails from school counselors, who in turn gave the letter to concerned parents looking for a way to talk with their own teens . . . .

Dear Johnny,

This fall you will be entering high school, and like most American teenagers, you'll have to navigate drugs. As most parents, I would prefer that you not use drugs. However, I realize that despite my wishes, you might experiment.

I will not use scare tactics to deter you. Instead, having spent the past 25 years researching drug use, abuse and policy, I will tell you a little about what I have learned, hoping this will lead you to make wise choices. My only concern is your health and safety.

When people talk about "drugs," they are generally referring to illegal substances such as marijuana, cocaine, methamphetamine (speed), psychedelic drugs (LSD, Ecstasy, "Shrooms") and heroin. These are not the only drugs that make you high. Alcohol, cigarettes and many other substances (like glue) cause intoxication of some sort. The fact that one drug or another is illegal does not mean one is better or worse for you. All of them temporarily change the way you perceive things and the way you think.

Some people will tell you that drugs feel good, and that's why they use them. But drugs are not always fun. Cocaine and methamphetamine speed up your heart; LSD can make you feel disoriented; alcohol intoxication impairs driving; cigarette smoking leads to addiction and sometimes lung cancer; and people sometimes die suddenly from taking heroin. Marijuana does not often lead to physical dependence or overdose, but it does alter the way people think, behave and react.

I have tried to give you a short description of the drugs you might encounter. I choose not to try to scare you by distorting information because I want you to have confidence in what I tell you. Although I won't lie to you about their effects, there are many reasons for a person your age to not use drugs or alcohol. First, being high on marijuana or any other drug often interferes with normal life. It is difficult to retain information while high, so using it, especially daily, affects your ability to learn.

Second, if you think you might try marijuana, please wait until you are older. Adults with drug problems often started using at a very early age.

Finally, your father and I don't want you to get into trouble. Drug and alcohol use is illegal for you, and the consequences of being caught are huge. Here in the United States, the number of arrests for possession of marijuana has more than doubled in the past six years. Adults are serious about "zero tolerance." If caught, you could be arrested, expelled from school, barred from playing sports, lose your driver's license, denied a college loan, and/or rejected from college.

Despite my advice to abstain, you may one day choose to experiment. I will say again that this is not a good idea, but if you do, I urge you to learn as much as you can, and use common sense. There are many excellent books and references, including the Internet, that give you credible information about drugs. You can, of course, always talk to me. If I don't know the answers to your questions, I will try to help you find them.

If you are offered drugs, be cautious. Watch how people behave, but understand that everyone responds differently even to the same substance. If you do decide to experiment, be sure you are surrounded by people you can count upon. Plan your transportation and under no circumstances drive or get into a car with anyone else who has been using alcohol or other drugs. Call us or any of our close friends any time, day or night, and we will pick you up, no questions asked and no consequences.

And please, Johnny, use moderation. It is impossible to know what is contained in illegal drugs because they are not regulated. The majority of fatal overdoses occur because young people do not know the strength of the drugs they consume, or how they combine with other drugs. Please do not participate in drinking contests, which have killed too many young people. Whereas marijuana by itself is not fatal, too much can cause you to become disoriented and sometimes paranoid. And of course, smoking can hurt your lungs, later in life and now.

Johnny, as your father and I have always told you about a range of activities (including sex), think about the consequences of your actions before you act. Drugs are no different. Be skeptical and, most of all, be safe.

Love, Mom

# Periodical Bibliography

The following articles have been selected to supplement the diverse views presented in this chapter.

Paul Armentano    "Testing Students for Drugs Is Neither Solution nor Bargain," *Fort Wayne (IN) New Sentinel,* September 21, 2005.

Arthur Bosse    "Designing Effective Youth Prevention Programming," *Addiction Professional,* March 2005.

Kelly N. Graves et al.    "Risk and Protective Factors Associated with Alcohol, Cigarette, and Marijuana Use During Adolescence," *Journal of Youth and Adolescence,* August 2005.

Robb London    "Is the War on Drugs Succeeding?" *Harvard Law Bulletin,* Summer 2005.

Renee Moilanen    "Marihuana: Just Say No Again; The Old Failures of New and Improved Anti-Drug Education," *Reason,* January 2004.

Bonita Reinert et al.    "Anti-Tobacco Messages from Different Sources Make a Difference with Secondary School Students," *Journal of Public Health Management and Practice,* November/December 2004.

Marsha Rosenbaum    "DARE: The Never-Ending Folly," *Orange County Register,* April 14, 2005.

John P. Walters    "Random Student Drug Testing Works: It's About Public Health—Identifying Individuals Who Need Help and Treatment—Not Punishment," *Pittsburgh Post-Gazette,* May 4, 2005.

# For Further Discussion

## Chapter 1

1.  According to Carolyn Banta and Donna Leinwand, teens are turning away from street drugs and, instead, are using household medicines and substances to get high. In your opinion, why might teens be more attracted to household drugs than they are to illicit drugs? Cite from the text to support your answer.

2.  Scott Burns argues that marijuana is a gateway drug that leads to the use of harder drugs such as heroin and cocaine. Based on your reading of the viewpoint, do you believe marijuana is a gateway drug? Why or why not?

3.  After your reading of the viewpoints presented in this chapter, which drugs pose the greatest risks to teens, in your opinion? Why? Cite from the viewpoints while constructing your answer.

## Chapter 2

1.  The Citizens Commission on Human Rights asserts that addiction is not a brain disease. Does this viewpoint identify the credentials and organizational affiliations of the psychiatrists and psychologists whose studies are offered in support of this premise? Why or why not, in your opinion?

2.  As of January 2006, eleven states have passed laws allowing the use of marijuana for health-related purposes, and the issue of legalization or decriminalization of the drug continues to draw controversy. Based on your reading of the viewpoints expressed by Karen P. Tandy, Karen O'Keefe, and Mitch Earleywine, is this debate science-based? Or is it politically motivated? Explain your answer using evidence from the texts.

3. Most people would agree that individuals with serious drug addictions should have access to medical treatment to break the dependency. Based on your reading of the arguments by Judy Shepps Battle and Maia Szalavitz, why is the discussion of drug abuse treatment for teens a controversial issue? With which author do you find yourself in agreement? Why?

## Chapter 3

1. Several viewpoints in this chapter address the question of how exposure to advertising affects the smoking and drinking behavior of teens. Based on the arguments presented here, do you believe advertisers have any obligation to help counteract underage smoking or drinking? Why or why not?

2. Jacob Sullum and the researchers from the Dartmouth Medical School disagree on whether movies have any significant influence on the smoking behavior of adolescents. Based on your reading of these viewpoints, which do you think is likely to have more impact on viewer behavior: the number of exposures to images of smoking, or the ways in which smoking is portrayed? Provide examples from the viewpoints to support your answer.

## Chapter 4

1. The U.S. Supreme Court has ruled that the drug testing of students participating in extracurricular activities is constitutional. Based on the arguments for and against drug testing presented in this chapter by Calvina L. Fay, John R. Knight, and Sharon Levy, what is your opinion on school-based drug testing? Should schools be allowed to test only students who participate in sports or other extracurricular activities? Should all students be subject to testing? Or should drug testing be eliminated from schools altogether?

2. Jay Mathews and Marsha Rosenbaum disagree about whether or not teens should be taught to drink responsibly by being served alcohol under the supervision of their parents. Based on your reading of their viewpoints, which position do you think is more appropriate for parents to take, the "zero-tolerance" perspective on drinking, or the "harm reduction" approach? Explain your answer.

# Organizations to Contact

**American Council for Drug Education (ACDE)**
164 W. Seventy-fourth St., New York, NY   10023
(800) 488-DRUG (3748) • fax: (212) 595-2553
Web site: www.acde.org

The American Council for Drug Education informs the public about the harmful effects associated with drug and alcohol abuse. It gives the public access to scientifically based prevention programs and materials. ACDE has resources for parents, youth, educators, prevention professionals, employers, health care professionals, and other concerned community members who are working to help America's youth avoid drug and alcohol abuse. ACDE is affiliated with Phoenix House, a nonprofit substance abuse services organization with one hundred programs in nine states.

**Canadian Centre on Substance Abuse (CCSA)**
75 Albert St., Suite 300, Ottawa, ON   K1P 5E7
    Canada
(613) 235-4048 • fax: (613) 235-8101
e-mail: admin@ccsa.ca
Web site: www.ccsa.ca

Established in 1988 by an act of Parliament, CCSA works to minimize the harm associated with the use of alcohol, tobacco, and other drugs. It disseminates information on the nature, extent, and consequences of substance abuse; publishes reports about youth substance abuse and community efforts to prevent and treat teen drug abuse; sponsors public debates on the topic; and supports organizations involved in substance abuse treatment, prevention, and educational programming. The centre publishes the newsletter *Action News* four times a year.

**Canadian Foundation for Drug Policy (CFDP)**
70 MacDonald St., Ottawa, ON   K2P 1H6
    Canada

(613) 236-1027 • fax: (613) 238-2891
e-mail: eoscapel@cfdp.ca
Web site: www.cfdp.ca

Founded by several of Canada's leading drug policy specialists, CFDP examines the objectives and consequences of Canada's drug laws and policies, including laws prohibiting marijuana use. When necessary, the foundation recommends alternatives that it believes would make Canada's drug policy issues more effective and humane. CFDP discusses drug policy issues with the Canadian government, media, and general public. It also disseminates educational materials and maintains a Web site.

## Cato Institute

1000 Massachusetts Ave. NW, Washington, DC 20001-5403
(202) 842-0200
e-mail: cato@cato.org
Web site: www.cato.org

The Cato Institute is a public policy research foundation dedicated to limiting the control of government and to protecting individual liberty. Cato, which strongly favors drug legalization, publishes the *Cato Journal* three times a year and the *Cato Policy Report* newsletter bimonthly. The institute also publishes policy studies on a variety of topics and approximately a dozen books each year.

## Center on Alcohol Marketing and Youth (CAMY)

Georgetown University, Washington, DC 20007
(202) 687-1019
Web site: www.camy.org

The Center on Alcohol Marketing and Youth monitors the marketing practices of the alcohol industry to focus attention on industry practices that jeopardize the health and safety of America's youth. CAMY is supported by grants to Georgetown University from the Pew Charitable Trusts and the Robert Wood Johnson Foundation.

**Drug Policy Alliance**
Office of Public Policy, New York, NY   10018
(212) 613-8020 • fax: (212) 613-8021
e-mail: nyc@drugpolicy.org
Web site: www.drugpolicy.org

The Drug Policy Alliance, an independent nonprofit organization created in 2000 when the Lindesmith Center merged with
the Drug Policy Foundation, supports and publicizes alternatives to current U.S policies on illegal drugs, including
marijuana. The organization's publications include the weekly
*Drug Policy Project Newsletter* and the book *The Great Drug
War*. The alliance sponsors Safety First, a drug education
program that advocates the harm-reduction approach to curb-
ing teen drug use.

**Drug Watch International (DWI)**
PO Box 45218, Omaha, NE   68145-0218
(402) 384-9212
Web site: www.drugwatch.org

Drug Watch International is a nonprofit, volunteer network
and advocacy organization that promotes drug-free cultures
worldwide and strongly opposes any legalization of drugs. The
organization defines its purpose as providing policy makers,
the media, and the public with current information, factual
research, and expert resources to counter drug advocacy
propaganda. DWI takes a comprehensive approach to the drug
issue through activities that promote drug use prevention,
education, intervention/treatment, and law enforcement/
interdiction.

**Family Research Council**
801 G St. NW, Washington, DC   20001
(202) 393-2100 • fax: (202) 393-2134
e-mail: corrdept@frc.org
Web site: www.frc.org

The council analyzes issues affecting the family and seeks to
protect the interests of the traditional family in the formula-
tion of public policy. It lobbies legislators and promotes public

debate on issues concerning the family. The council publishes articles and position papers against the legalization of medicinal marijuana.

## Harm Reduction Coalition
22 W. Twenty-seventh St., 5th Floor., New York, NY   10001
(212) 213-6376
e-mail: hrc@harmreduction.org

The coalition is a nationwide network of people and organizations that are committed to reducing drug-related harm to individuals and communities. Members include service providers, health-care workers, medical professionals, drug treatment specialists, researchers, policy makers, drug users and those with a history of drug use, and legal professionals, all of whom are involved in the creation and facilitation of effective harm-reduction services that provide alternatives to conventional health and human services, drug treatment programs, and "zero-tolerance" policies.

## The Heritage Foundation
214 Massachusetts Ave. NE, Washington, DC   20002-2302
(202) 546-4400 • fax: (202) 546-8328
e-mail: info@heritage.org
Web site: www.heritage.org

The Heritage Foundation is a conservative public policy research institute that opposes the legalization of drugs and advocates strengthening law enforcement to stop drug abuse. It publishes position papers on a broad range of topics, including drug issues. Its regular publications include the monthly *Policy Review*, the Backgrounder series of occasional papers, and the Heritage Lecture series.

## Marijuana Policy Project
PO Box 77492-Capitol Hill, Washington, DC   20013
(202) 462-5747 • fax: (202) 232-0442
e-mail: mpp@mpp.org
Web site: www.mpp.org

The Marijuana Policy Project develops and promotes policies to minimize the harms associated with marijuana. Its primary function is lobbying to reform marijuana laws on the federal level. The project increases public awareness through speaking engagements, educational seminars, the mass media, and briefing papers.

**National Center on Addiction and Substance Abuse at Columbia University (CASA)**
633 Third Ave., 19th Floor., New York, NY   10017-6706
(212) 841-5200
Web site: www.casacolumbia.org

Housed on the campus of Columbia University, CASA is a private, nonprofit organization that works to educate the public about the hazards of chemical dependency. The organization supports treatment as the best way to reduce chemical dependency. It produces publications describing the harmful effects of alcohol and drug addiction and effective ways to address the problem of substance abuse.

**National Clearinghouse for Alcohol and Drug Information**
PO Box 2345, Rockville, MD   20847-2345
(800) 729-6686
e-mail: shs@health.org
Web site: www.health.org

The clearinghouse distributes publications of the U.S. Department of Health and Human Services, the National Institute on Drug Abuse, and other federal agencies concerned with alcohol and drug abuse. Brochure titles include *Tips for Teens About Marijuana.*

**National Institute on Drug Abuse (NIDA)**
National Institutes of Health, Bethesda, MD   20892-9561
(301) 443-1124
e-mail: information@nida.nih.gov
Web site: www.nida.nih.gov

NIDA supports and conducts research on drug abuse—including the yearly Monitoring the Future Survey—to improve addiction prevention, treatment, and policy efforts. It publishes the bimonthly *NIDA Notes* newsletter, the periodic "InfoFacts" fact sheets, and a catalog of research reports and public education materials, such as *Marijuana: Facts for Teens* and *Marijuana: Facts Parents Need to Know.*

### National Organization for the Reform of Marijuana Laws (NORML)
1600 K St. NW, Suite 501, Washington, DC   20006-2832
(202) 483-5500 • fax: (202) 483-0057
e-mail: norml@norml.org
Web site: www.norml.org

NORML fights to legalize marijuana and to help those who have been convicted and sentenced for possessing or selling marijuana. In addition to pamphlets and position papers, it publishes periodic newsletters and legislative bulletins and provides daily access to nationwide marijuana news headlines and articles through its Web site.

### NORML Canada
593-C Bank St., Ottawa, ON   K1S 3T4
   Canada
(604) 852-5110 • fax: (604) 859-3361
e-mail: norml@norml.ca
Web site: www.norml.ca

NORML Canada believes the discouragement of marijuana use through use of criminal law has been excessively costly and harmful to both society and individuals. A nonprofit public interest organization chartered at the federal level since 1978, NORML Canada works at all levels of government to eliminate criminal penalties for private marijuana use.

### Office of National Drug Control Policy
Drug Policy Information Clearinghouse, Rockville, MD
   20849-6000
(800) 666-3332 • fax: (301) 519-5212

e-mail: ondcp@ncjrs.org
Web site: www.whitehousedrugpolicy.gov

The Office of National Drug Control Policy is responsible for formulating the government's national drug strategy and the president's antidrug policy as well as coordinating the federal agencies responsible for stopping drug trafficking. The ONDCP sponsors the National Youth Anti-Drug Media Campaign, which maintains a drug education Web site for parents (www.theantidrug.com), and one for teens (www.freevibe.com). Drug policy studies are available from the ONDCP upon request.

**Partnership for a Drug-Free America**
405 Lexington Ave., Suite 1601, New York, NY   10174
(212) 922-1560 • fax: (212) 922-1570
Web site: www.drugfree.org

The Partnership for a Drug-Free America is a nonprofit organization that utilizes media communication to reduce demand for illicit drugs in America. Best known for its national antidrug advertising campaigning, the partnership works to "unsell" drugs to children and to prevent drug use among kids. It publishes an annual report, the periodic *Partnership News* newsletter, a monthly e-newsletter for teens, and frequent news releases and bulletins about current events with which the partnership is involved.

**U.S. Drug Enforcement Administration (DEA)**
Mailstop: AES, 2401 Jefferson Davis Hwy., Alexandria, VA
    22301
(202) 307-1000
Web site: www.usdoj.gov/dea

The DEA is the federal agency charged with enforcing the nation's drug laws. The agency concentrates on stopping the smuggling of narcotics in the United States and abroad. It publishes the *Drug Enforcement Magazine* three times a year, and sponsors the "Think Twice" antidrug campaign at www. justthinktwice.com.

# Bibliography of Books

Nikki Babbit

*Adolescent Drug and Alcohol Abuse: How to Spot It, Stop It, and Get Help for Your Family*. Sebastapol, CA: O'Reilly, 2000.

Claudia Black

*Straight Talk from Claudia Black: What Recovering Parents Should Tell Their Kids About Drugs and Alcohol*. Center City, MN: Hazelden, 2003.

Arthur W. Blume

*Treating Drug Problems*. Hoboken, NJ: Wiley, 2005.

Alan Bock

*Waiting to Inhale: The Politics of Medical Marijuana*. Santa Ana, CA: Seven Locks Press, 2000.

Rosalyn Carson-DeWitt, ed.

*Drugs, Alcohol, and Tobacco: Learning About Addictive Behavior*. New York: Macmillan Reference USA, 2003.

Jonathan P. Caulkins et al.

*School-Based Drug Prevention: What Kind of Drug Use Does It Prevent?* Santa Monica, CA: Rand, 2002.

Rod Colvin

*Prescription Drug Addiction: The Hidden Epidemic*. Omaha, NE: Addicus Books, 2002.

Dennis M. Donovan and G. Alan Marlatt

*Assessment of Addictive Behaviors*. New York: Guilford, 2005.

Robert L. Dupont and Betty Ford

*The Selfish Brain: Learning from Addiction*. Washington, DC: Hazelden Information Education, 2000.

Mitch Earleywine

*Understanding Marijuana: A New Look at the Scientific Evidence*. New York: Oxford University Press, 2002.

Griffith Edwards — *Matters of Substance: Drugs—and Why Everyone's a User.* New York: Thomas Dunne, 2004.

Richard Fields — *Drugs in Perspective: A Personalized Look at Substance Use and Abuse.* New York: McGraw-Hill, 2004.

Paul Gahlinger — *Illegal Drugs.* New York: Penguin, 2004.

Victoria C. G. Greenleaf — *Fighting the Good Fight: One Family's Struggle Against Adolescent Alcoholism.* Fort Bragg, CA: Cypress House, 2002.

Carolyn Hilarski — *Addiction, Assessment, and Treatment with Adolescents, Adults, and Families.* Binghamton, NY: Haworth, 2005.

Institute of Medicine — *Reducing Underage Drinking: A Collective Responsibility.* Washington, DC: National Academies Press, 2004.

Denise B. Kandel, ed. — *Stages and Pathways of Drug Involvement: Examining the Gateway Hypothesis.* New York: Cambridge University Press, 2002.

Alison Mack and Janet Joy — *Marijuana as Medicine: The Science Beyond the Controversy.* Washington, DC: National Academies Press, 2000.

Bill Manville — *Cool, Hip, and Sober: 88 Ways to Beat Booze and Drugs.* New York: Tom Doherty Associates, 2003.

Shelly Marshall — *Young, Sober, and Free: Experience, Strength, and Hope for Young Adults.* Center City, MN: Hazelden, 2003.

| | |
|---|---|
| Peter M. Monti, Suzanne Colby, and Tracy A. O'Leary | *Adolescents, Alcohol, and Substance Abuse: Reaching Teens.* New York, Guilford, 2001. |
| Drew Pinsky | *When Painkillers Become Dangerous: What Everyone Needs to Know About OxyContin and Other Prescription Drugs.* Center City, MN: Hazelden, 2004. |
| Jeffrey A. Schaler | *Addiction Is a Choice.* Peru, IL: Carus, 2000. |
| Sally J. Stevens and Andrew R. Morral | *Adolescent Substance Abuse Treatment in the United States: Exemplary Models from a National Evaluation Study.* Binghamton, NY: Haworth, 2003. |
| Victor C. Strasburger and Barbara J. Wilson | *Children, Adolescents, and the Media.* Thousand Oaks, CA: Sage, 2002. |
| Andrew T. Weil and Winifred Rosen | *From Chocolate to Morphine: Everything You Need to Know About Mind-Altering Drugs.* New York: Houghton Mifflin, 2004. |
| Bettie B. Youngs, Jennifer Leigh Youngs, and Tina Moreno | *A Teen's Guide to Living Drug Free.* Deerfield Beach, FL: Health Communications, 2003. |
| Koren Zailckas | *Smashed: Story of a Drunken Girlhood.* New York: Penguin, 2005. |

# Index

sexual attitudes/behavior, 142
sexual enhancers, 62, 65
Shih, Chuan-Fong, 157
Siegel, Michael, 153, 154, 157
silver spray paint, 62
Simmons Market Research
  Bureau, Inc., 156
Smoke Free Movies campaign,
  167
smokeless tobacco, 146–47,
  149–50
smoking
    cigarette companies need
      teen, 147
    deterrents to prevent onset
      of, 159–60
    media influence on, 142
    *see also* movies, smoking in;
      tobacco advertising; tobacco
      use
"snappers," 62
Souder, Mark, 119
Sowell, Thomas, 99, 100, 102–103
spray paints, 62
stimulants, 25
STOP Underage Drinking Act, 38
Strattera, 105
student athletes, 186
student drug testing. *See* drug
  testing
substance abuse
    experimentation versus,
      19–21
    statistics on, 203
    weak family and school ties
      linked to, 183
    *see also* drug abuse; substance
      use
Substance Abuse and Mental
  Health Services Administration
  (SAMHSA), 23, 97, 121, 127,
  130
substance use
    booklet giving advice to
      parents on, 196–98

conversion to addiction from,
  30–31
historical changes in, 25
substance abuse and addiction versus, 19–21
*see also* alcohol use; drug use
"sudden sniffing death," 65–66
suffocation, 66
Sullivan, Fran, 71–72
Sullum, Jacob, 155, 165
Sweden, 41–42
Switzerland, 112
Szalavitz, Maia, 126
Szasz, Thomas, 86, 87

Tandy, Karen P., 106
television
    affecting real-life behavior,
      141–42
    amount of time spent view-
      ing, 141
    antismoking campaign on,
      157
tetrahydrocannabinol (THC), 48,
  110, 113
"Texas shoe-shine," 62
thefts, of cough and cold
  medicine, 75
"The Sober Truth on Preventing
  Underage Drinking Act"
  (STOP), 36, 38
Titus-Ernstoff, Linda, 164
tobacco advertising
    aimed at teens
      continuance of, 145–46
      evidence of link between
        smoking and, 147–50
      tobacco industry state-
        ments and actions on,
        144–45
    ban on
      antismoking messages
        instead of, 158–59